MUSCLE CARS

THE LEGEND LIVES ON

igloo

This edition published 2007

First published in 2005
by Igloo Books Ltd
Cottage Farm,
Sywell,
NN6 OBJ
www.igloo-books.com

ISBN 978-1-84561-253-5

10 9 7 8 6 5 4

Project management: Kandour Ltd
Editor: Nik Berg
Art Director: Susan Holmes
Contributors: Mark Holmes, Ivan Berg
Production: Kaspa Hazlewood & Karen Lomax
Picture Editor: Peter Trafford

Images supplied courtesy of: DaimlerChrysler, Ford, General Motors, Motoring Picture Library
Special thanks to: Larry Kinsel, Randy Jacobs, Brandt Rosenbusch, Jon Day

Printed in China

MUSCLE CARS

THE LEGEND LIVES ON

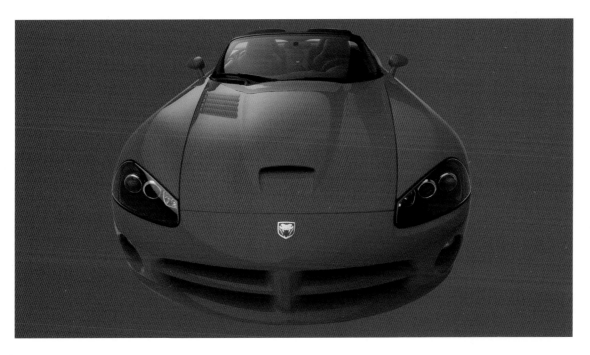

Nik Berg

igloo

Contents

Introduction

It's the sheer simplicty of the Muscle Car that makes it so universally appealing. The recipe is just so straightforward. Take a compact automobile and install an incredibly-powerful engine (preferably a V8) to deliver a tire-frying performance. No auto enthusiast can argue with that one. It's a formula for success that has been tried and tested for 50 years and has created some of the most exciting cars in history. Just mentioning the names Mustang, Charger, GTO, Corvette or Viper sends a shiver down the spine.

The Muscle Car story began in America's post-war boom of the 1950s as inter-brand rivalry in Detroit saw horsepower figures steadily rising through the decade. But these big engines were being fitted to big cars and they didn't have mass-market appeal.

That would all change in 1964 when Pontiac installed a full-size engine into a mid-size car and created the awesome GTO, the first true Muscle Car. And the rest of Detroit followed. Fast. The Ford Mustang, Plymouth Road Runner, Dodge Charger, Plymouth Barracuda and Chevrolet Camaro all appeared before the eager public could pause for breath. Horsepower went through the roof as the cars competed on the streets and on the track. Ford managed to wring 675bhp out of its Cammer V8, the highest power of any Detroit engine ever. Hertz bought up a whole series of Shelby GT350 Mustangs to rent out to weekend racers and Plymouth's Road Runner Superbird and its Dodge Daytona rival brought NASCAR to the streets. It was Muscle Car mania.

But dark clouds were looming. Tough emissions rules and the oil crisis forced automobile manufacturers to rethink. Power outputs fell through the floor during the 1970s and there were plenty of casualties. The Dodge Charger and Challenger, Plymouth Road Runner and Pontiac GTO all fell victim to the

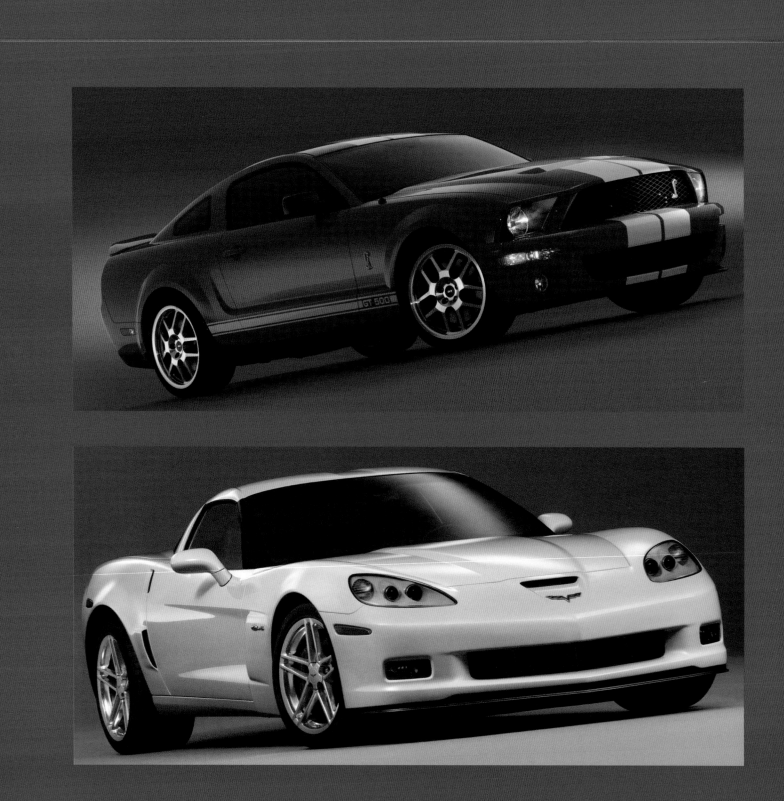

legislation and it looked like the Muscle Car was dead.

Only Pontiac's Firebird Trans Am, Chevrolet's Camaro and Corvette and Ford's Mustang kept the spirit alive. But the truth was that for many years these cars were anything but muscular, offering a lot more show than go.

It was only towards the very end of the 1980s that things were looking up. The survivors were beginning to pack more punch and at least one company was reminiscing about the good old days.

That company was Chrysler. In a bid to re-establish its Dodge and Plymouth brands the designers and engineers had been studying their history. In 1989 the Detroit Auto Show ground to a halt as the wraps came off the Dodge Viper concept car. With its epic V10 engine and muscular lines it was the machine that Muscle Car fans had been dreaming of for two decades.

Dodge put the Viper into production and it was a phenomenal hit. Come 1997 the company was ready to do it again, this time with the Plymouth Prowler – a hot rod for the 21st Century. Performance and style were hot again.

Today Muscle Cars are back with a vengeance and legendary names are reappearing in dealerships, drag strips and ovals. The 2005 C6 Corvette is the most powerful ever, packing 500bhp in S06 trim. Chrysler has brought back the 300 and the Dodge Charger. Ford has revived the Mustang Shelby GT500. It's like the glory days of the 1960s all over again.

The Muscle Cars of the new millennium are faster than ever before and not just able to rip up the quarter-mile, but relish twisty roads too with advanced suspension and the latest electronic driver aids. If that sounds too complicated for die hard Muscle Car fans don't worry, because none of the newcomers has forgotten that basic principle. Horsepower is still the number one priority as the Muscle Car legend lives on.

AMC AMX

AMC's cut-down Javelin was an oddball, but it was the company's best player in the muscle car era

The AMC AMX of 1968 was a unique proposition. It was the only two-seater American sportscar of the time.

Essentially a cut-down version of AMC's Javelin the AMX (American Motors eXperimental), was a foot shorter than its sibling. Its proportions were rather odd, but the AMX was significantly lighter than the Javelin.

And with the top-flight 315bhp 390 cubic inch V8 installed, the AMX was a lively performer. Zero to sixty came in just 6.9 seconds and the quarter-mile in 15 seconds. There was a four-speed manual tranny, toughened suspension and bucket seats for the two occupants. A 290 and 343 V8 were lesser options.

Land speed racing legend Craig Breedlove set no less than 106 speed records with an AMX in February 1968 and, to celebrate, a special run of 50 Craig Breedlove editions were built. Finished in patriotic red, white and blue, few survive today.

A few minor cosmetic changes were made for 1969 but the year is best remembered for the Big Bad AMX, available in bold orange, green and blue color schemes with matching bumpers.

Also offered was a Go pack to include power disc brakes, uprated suspension for improved handling and redline tires.

A very limited run of SS cars designed for the drag strip were also produced. Modifications to the 390 cubic inch V8 engine resulted in a claimed power output of 340bhp, but as was frequently the case in the muscle car era, this was a very conservative estimate. The SS package almost doubled the AMX's sticker price, so it's unsurprising that only around 50 were sold.

MODEL HISTORY

1968
AMX launched, based on shortened Javelin

1969
Limited-run SS is the most powerful and most expensive AMX

1970
The last two-seater AMX is built

1971
AMX is now the top model in the Javelin range

1974
AMX production run ends

1970 saw the last of the real two-seater AMX models. Little was changed, but a ram air induction scoop was added to make the hood more aggressive.

In 1971 the AMC AMX ceased to be a model in its own right and was the name for the top model Javelin. Under the curiously-bulbous hood was a choice of two 360 cubic inch V8s with 245 or 290bhp.

More power came with the Go package which slotted a 401 330bhp V8 under the hood and upgraded the wheels, tires and brakes as part of the deal.

1972 would be the last year for the AMX as a muscle car. The Go package was still available but the entry-level engine had been reduced to a 304 cubic inch unit with a paltry 150bhp.

The AMX continued to be sold until 1974, but its days as a muscle car were long finished.

Specification

Years built	1966-1974
Most powerful model	1969 SS
Engine type	V8
Displacement	401 cid
Transmission	four-speed manual
Power	340bhp
Top speed	120mph

The AMX of 1968 was a unique proposition. It was the only two-seater American sportscar of the time

Buick Gran Sport

Buick's entry to the muscle car fray may have been late but it was a worthy contender

Pontiac's success with its 1964 GTO was the spur for Buick to produce the GS. Many consider the GTO as the first true muscle car, setting the formula for others to follow: drop a big-block V8 into an intermediate-sized car and sell it at a budget price.

So Buick shoehorned its 401 cubic inch 'nailhead' V8 into its existing Skylark model, bestowing it with 325bhp, to cash in on this new trend. The 1965 Skylark Gran Sport wasn't as big a hit as the GTO, but it started a model line that would develop truly muscular looks and performance. Despite arriving a bit late in the day, the Gran Sport was a strong seller in its first year and Buick was encouraged to hone the car further.

For 1966, the Gran Sport was treated to a new, hotter 340bhp version of the 401 engine, dropping its quarter mile time by a second to 15.4secs. But buying into the Buick brand wasn't cheap and Gran Sport sales were a lot slower than in its introductory year.

The name was abbreviated in 1967, when the GS 400 arrived with a new, higher-revving 400 cid engine also giving 340bhp. A new three-speed auto transmission and the 260bhp 'junior' GS 340 also saw the light of day and its cut price helped sales.

Through '68 and '69 the GS was weighed down by huge chrome fenders, but an interseting option quietly appeared at dealerships. The Stage One Special Package came with a unique 400 cid motor. Although officially rated at 345bhp (just 5bhp more than the regular 400), the reality was more like 390bhp. In 1969 a Stage Two option came with an official 360bhp.

MODEL HISTORY

1965
Buick fits 401 cid 'nailhead' engine into Skylark, producing the Gran Sport

1967
New 400 cid V8 introduced, along with the smaller-engined GS 340

1969
Previously fake hood scoops became a functional part of the induction system

1970
The GS 455 is born. In Stage 1 tune with the GSX style pack, it is the ultimate Buick muscle car

1972
Last true Buick GS produced. After this the name became a pale shadow of its former glory

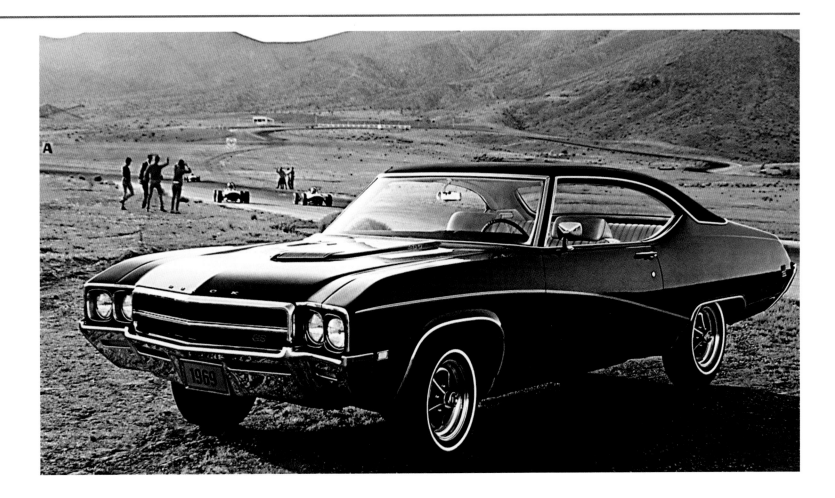

In 1970, the GS reached its pinnacle. That year's GS 455 had a brand new 455 cubic inch engine to give plenty of go, while the GSX appearance package provided all the show: spoilers, classic body stripes and supersize tires.

The combination made for the ultimate Buick muscle car of all time, when the Stage 1 performance package was specified, giving a hotter cam, bigger valves and a revised carburetor. The company under-rated it at 360bhp, as road testers of the time claimed it was nearer 400bhp!

Along with its high-performance brethren, 1971 signalled the beginning of the end for the GS, with the introduction of low-lead gasoline lowering power and higher insurance premiums turning buyers away. Post-1972, the GS name was shunted from one Buick coupe to another, the glory of the muscle car years long gone, and in 1975 it ceased to exist.

Specification

Years built	1965 to 1975
Most powerful model	1970 GS 455
Engine type	V8
Displacement	455 cu in
Transmission	three-speed automatic
Power	360bhp
Top speed	130mph

The company under-rated it at 360bhp, as road testers of the time claimed it was nearer 400bhp

Buick Wildcat

Buick's first attempt at high-performance never shrugged of its luxury image

Buick was not a company with a reputation for high performance machinery, but that all started to change in 1962 when the Wildcat hit the scene.

Part of the Invicta line, the Wildcat Sport Coupe (as it was officially called) benefited from a beefed-up chassis and suspension, and more dragstrip-oriented transmission ratios to make the most of the 401 cid V8 engine's 325bhp. It also came loaded with luxury, which helped to pump its weight up to a hefty 4,150 pounds.

During its eight-year lifespan, the Wildcat was bestowed with more and more power. The original two-door hardtop body style was also bolstered by a four-door hardtop, a two-door convertible and finally a conventional four-door sedan.

Despite Buick's view of the Wildcat as a sports car, the public thought different and it was the staid-looking sedan that saw the greatest sales success.

In '64, two new optional 425 cid V8s were made available, with 340 and 360bhp, which helped to offset the increased 4,500-pound curb weight.

The turning point in terms of styling was 1965, which saw the Wildcat sharing its sheet metal with its Buick stablemate, the Le Sabre, and losing some of its individuality in the process.

The introduction of the Wildcat Custom, with more luxurious interior trimming, arrived in 1966 along with an optional high performance package. Only 21 owners are known to have signed up for this high-performance 425 cid V8, which was good for 380bhp and 465 lbft of torque

MODEL HISTORY

1962
First Wildcat introduced as part of Buick's Invicta model line-up powered by 325bhp 401 cid V8

1963
Sports coupe body style is augmented by a four-door hardtop and two-door convertible

1964
Optional 340 and 360bhp 425 cid V8s introduced, along with new four-door sedan

1965
All-new styling sees Wildcat sharing bodywork with Buick Le Sabre

1970
Final model has most powerful standard engine at 370bhp

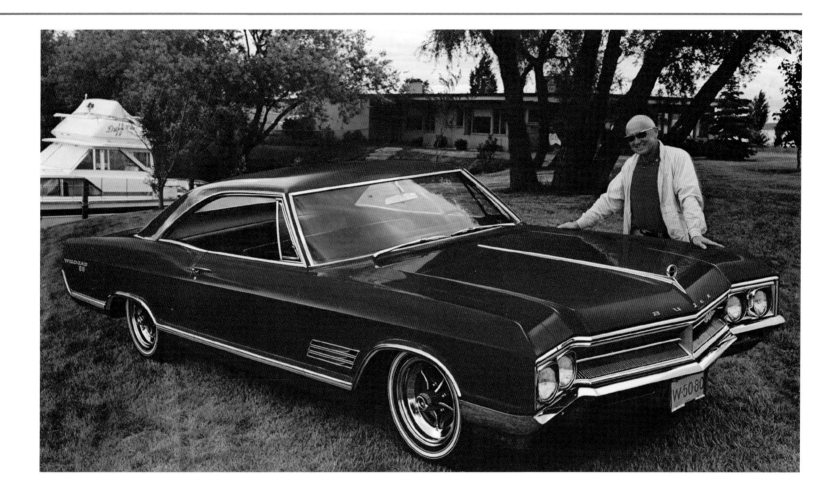

thanks to a pair of four-barrel carbs and a dual exhaust making the gas flow freely.

A more efficient domed combustion chamber in the all-new standard 430 cid engine of 1967 raised power to 360bhp, but by '69 the styling was so similar to the Le Sabre that the two were virtually identical. Only the grille, a few body moldings and the steering wheel differentiated between the two, and the Wildcat's lack of identity led to a drop in sales.

The end came in 1970, but the Wilcat went out with a howl, not a whimper. The run-out model featured Buick's all-new 455 cid V8, producing 370bhp and and 510 lbft of torque.

So what was arguably Buick's first performance car ended its days with the most powerful standard engine it ever had.

The flirtation with muscle cars was a short one and Buick reverted to what its buyers loved best; luxury.

Specification

Years built	1962 to 1970
Most powerful model	1970 455
Engine type	V8
Displacement	455 cu in
Transmission	three-speed automatic
Power	370bhp
Top speed	130mph

The flirtation with muscle cars was a short one and Buick reverted to what its buyers loved best

Chevrolet Camaro

Chevrolet's answer to the Ford Mustang came a bit late, but it was worth the wait

The Camaro was General Motors' belated response to the Mustang. Two years after Ford's pony car appeared GM released the Camaro. Those two years hadn't been wasted though, and the 1967 Camaro was an instant success.

It came as a hardtop coupe and convertible and could be tailored to each individual customer's requirements. There were four engines, a choice of three basic trim packages and no less than 80 factory options and a further 40 dealer options. It took longer to browse the brochure than to build the car!

As standard the Camaro came with a 230 cubic inch straight six with 140bhp or a 250 with 155bhp, but of far more interest were the V8s. A 327 came with 295bhp or 275bhp and there was a 350 offered as part of the SS package with 325bhp and then a 396 with 375bhp. The SS also offered

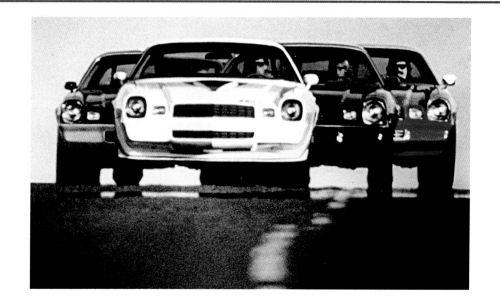

There were no less than 80 factory options and a further 40 dealer options. It took longer to browse the brochure than to build the car

1967 SS pace car (opposite), '79 cars (above) and '69 on the beach (right)

unique bumble bee stripes, air intakes on the hood and a blacked out grille. To make your Camaro stand out even further there was the RS pack which included hidden headlights, revised tail lamps and a higher level of interior trim. You could even combine the two packages to get performance with style with an RS/SS. Adding further credibility was the Camaro's role as pace car for the 1967 Indy 500.

By the end of the year there was another option: the Z-28. It's a name that would soon become synonymous with serious street performance, but initially the car wasn't even listed in the brochure or advertised.

The Z-28 was a homologation special, built so that the Camaro could go racing in the Trans Am Series, and although its 302 cubic inch motor was officially rated at just 290bhp, the truth was that this

MUSCLE CARS

MODEL HISTORY

1967
Chevrolet launches the Camaro – two years after the Ford Mustang

1969
The most powerful Camaros appear. First the COPO 427 with 450bhp and then the ZL1 with 500bhp

1970
The second generation arrives with European-influenced styling

1971
GM's new regulations strangle power outputs

1980
Power outputs drop throughout the decade, leaving a Z-28 with just 165bhp

engine threw out closer to 400bhp. Mated to a four-speed manual Muncie transmission and with power disc front brakes and competition suspension there was no mistaking this car's breeding. But just in case you wanted to drum the message home you could add a set of racing stripes.

With a top speed of 140mph the Z-28 was a spectacular way to celebrate the end of 1967 and ring in the new year.

Revisions for 1968 centred on some minor styling changes and uprating the rear suspension to multi-leaf springs, but 1969 would be a big year for the Camaro.

First came a restyle to give the car a wider and lower stance plus there was a new dashboard and seats.

However, the biggest changes were under the hood. SS customers could opt for one of two ram air systems – one was an aggressive new hood, with a rear-facing air inlet and the other, if you didn't want that power bulge on the bonnet, was a dealer-fit plenum kit.

A new 307 V8 was offered with a modest 200bhp but for extreme performance Chevrolet offered a mighty 427 cub inch unit.

First there was a dealer-fit engine that offered up to 450bhp. Ordered through Chevrolet's Central Office Production Order System these COPO were installed by well-known dealers including Yenko Sports Cars of Pennsylvania. Yenko also added rallye wheels and upgraded suspension to create their ultimate Camaro.

But even these COPO cars were put in the shade by Chevrolet's own ZL1. This aluminium block engine was rated at 430bhp but was really closer to 500bhp. Designed to compete in NHRA Super Stock drag racing, only a handful were sold as the cost of the engine alone nearly doubled the price of the car.

1970 saw the birth of the second generation. It had a more rounded European look and was notably much more refined

For extreme performance Chevrolet offered a mighty 427 cubic inch engine

1982
The third incarnation is launched with an embarrassing 90bhp engine as standard

1985
IROC-Z is unveiled and boosts power to 215bhp

1993
The final generation appears. Z28 offers 275bhp

1997
30th anniversary celebrated with a 330bhp SS LT1

2003
Camaro production ends

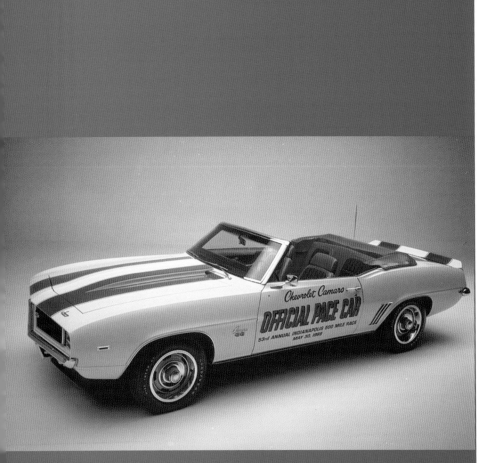

than the first Camaros.

Engines were carried over, although the 396 actually now displaced 402 cubic inches, and the Z-28 received a 350 LT1 engine with 360bhp.

1971 was a bad year for GM muscle cars and the Camaro's horsepower was slashed thanks to emissions regulations. Even the Z-28 was down to 330bhp.

Throughout the 1970s the Camaro's styling was revised to incorporate new Federal bumpers and power steadily declined. By the end of the mark two's production run a California-spec Z-28 had a paltry 165bhp.

In 1982 the third incarnation appeared. More angular styling and an all-new chassis with new suspension were the highlights.

1996 coupe (below) and 35th anniversary specials from 1992 (opposite)

Under the bonnet it was a bit of a disappointment. The entry-level engine was a 2.5-liter (153 cubic inch) four-cylinder unit with a pathetic 90bhp, then there was a 2.8-liter (171 cid) V6 with 112bhp and even the highest rated five-liter (305 cid) V8 had

THE ULTIMATE
CAMARO

1969 was undoubtedly the best year to buy a Camaro if you really felt the need for speed. COPO cars modified at big Chevy dealers such as Yenko in Pennsylvania, Nickey in Chicago, Dana in California and Baldwin-Motion in New York produced up to 450bhp. But the factory went further. To compete in the NHRA Super Stock drag class they needed to produce 50 road cars. Fitted with an aluminium block ZL1 engine officially rated at 430bhp, the truth was that this car had more like 500bhp. Even on street tyres and a standard exhaust it could run the standard quarter-mile in 13 seconds. In full race trim it was two seconds faster. But it was expensive. At $4,160 just the engine cost more than a standard SS model and only 69 were made.

just 165bhp. It was the lowest point in the Camaro's production history.

Over its ten-year life power did gradually pick up, though. In '85 came the IROC-Z with a more respectable 215bhp. And by 1992 this was boosted to 245bhp bringing some credibility back to the Camaro brand.

For its final generation the 1993 Camaro relaimed even more street cred. With its aerodynamic new design, revised suspension for improved handling and power levels that once again approached those of the 1970s it was the most accom-plished Camaro ever. Engines were a 3.4-liter (207 cid) 160bhp V6 or a 5.7-liter (348 cid) 275bhp V8 in the Z-28.

A convertible joined the coupe a year later and in 1996 the SS model returned with a bang, offering 305bhp. Then to celebrate the Camaro's 30th anniversary in 1997 it received the superb LS1 engine from the Corvette offering 330bhp and making it the most powerful model in over 20 years.

The Camaro carried on long enough to celebrate its 35th anniversary with another special edition but 2002 would mark the end for this once great muscle car.

Specification

Years built	1967 to 2002
Most powerful model	1967 COPO ZL1
Engine type	V8
Displacement	427 cu in
Transmission	four-speed manual, rear-wheel drive
Power	500bhp
Top speed	150mph

1969 coupe (above) and 1977 Z28 (right)

1988 T-Top (above) and 1981 Z28 (left)

2001 convertible (above) and 1993 T-Top (right),

*1994 Z28 (above)
and the 1987
collection (right)*

Chevrolet Chevelle SS

Chevy's response to the Pontiac GTO
soon overshadowed its rival

Initially outgunned by its rivals, the Chevrolet Chevelle SS actually went on to become one of the all time most powerful muscle cars.

Launched in 1964, the Chevelle SS was a fairly plain-looking sedan and , although a 283 cubic inch and 327 V8 were both offered and the maximum output was a sizeable 300bhp, it still fell a long way short of Pontiac's GTO.

Chevrolet reacted quickly and by 1965 the Z-16 Chevelle SS packed 375bhp from its 396 cubic inch V8. Now fiercely

fast, it could accelerate from 0-60mph in six seconds flat and do the standing quarter mile in less than 15 seconds.

Such was the pace of muscle car development that the Chevelle was redesigned a year later with a more rounded look and two bonnet scoops that would be a hallmark of the SS.

By 1968 the Chevelle had been redrawn again, with a more aggressive fastback body, although power remained at 375bhp from the highest-rated L78 V8.

But even that wasn't enough in the

MODEL HISTORY

1964

Chevelle SS launched, but lacks punch

1965

Problem solved thanks to the 375bhp Z-16

1968

Major restyle brings a fastback body

1970

Chevelle becomes the most powerful muscle car ever with 450bhp

1973

Chevelle production run ends

Muscle Car Wars, so in '69 Chevrolet released a limited number of very special Chevelles. Known as the COPO (Central Office Production Order) cars they packed even more punch from a special order engine that was catalogued as the L72.

1970 was the Chevelle's finest hour, though. In went a 402 or 454 cubic inch motor, with the LS6 454 unit producing an epic 450bhp. It was the fastest SS ever and could do the standing quarter-mile in less than 14 seconds.

But sadly it wasn't to last. Having to run on unleaded fuel and meet tough new emissions standards set by GM management meant that the great V8s were strangled and even the highest output engine was down almost 100bhp on the previous year.

It was a big come down for a once great car and sales dropped by almost two thirds. By 1973 the Chevelle SS was gone.

Specification

Years built	1964 to 1973
Most powerful model	1970 SS
Engine type	V8
Displacement	454 cu in
Transmission	four-speed manual
Power	450bhp
Top speed	130mph

1970 was the Chevelle's finest hour. In went a 454 cubic inch motor producing an epic 450bhp

Chevrolet Corvette

The Chevrolet Corvette has been America's Sports Car for more than 50 years

Now in its sixth generation the Chevrolet Corvette has been America's Sports Car for more than 50 years.

Unlike many of the machines on these pages, the 'Vette was designed as a sports car from the word go. Over the years it has become ever more sophisticated but, like a WWF wrestler in a hand-cut suit, there's never been any mistaking its true purpose.

Originally shown as a concept car at the General Motors Motorama at New York's Waldorf Astoria hotel in January of 1953, it was launched to the public barely six months later.

Penned by legendary GM stylist Harley Earl, the Corvette was undoubtedly a thing of beauty. It was compact and cute and featured some of Earl's best known party pieces including 'twin pod' rear fenders and 'rocket ship' tail lights as well as a snarling toothy grille. Initially only available in Polo

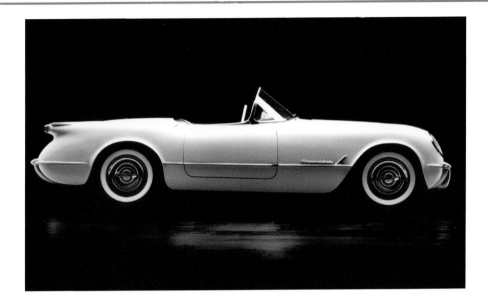

Originally shown as a concept car, it was launched to the public barely six months later

1972 Stingray (opposite page) 1953 original (top) and 1960 convertible (right)

White with a red interior, the Corvette was drop dead georgeous.

It also marked a radical departure in production methods. All Corvettes were hand built, based on a shortened Chevrolet passenger car chassis of 102 inches and with those beautiful curves created not from beaten metal, but moulded fiberglass. The 'Vette boasted coil sprung wishbone suspension at the front and four-leaf semi-elliptical springs at the rear end.

Under the hood was an off-the-shelf 235 cubic inch straight six engine, tricked up with a higher lift cam to produce 150bhp. Chevy's Powerglide two-speed auto transmission was fitted as standard.

The 'Vette is one of the biggest success stories in American automobile history, but it actually got off to a very rocky start. The hand-built Corvette commanded a hand-built price. In fact it cost more than a

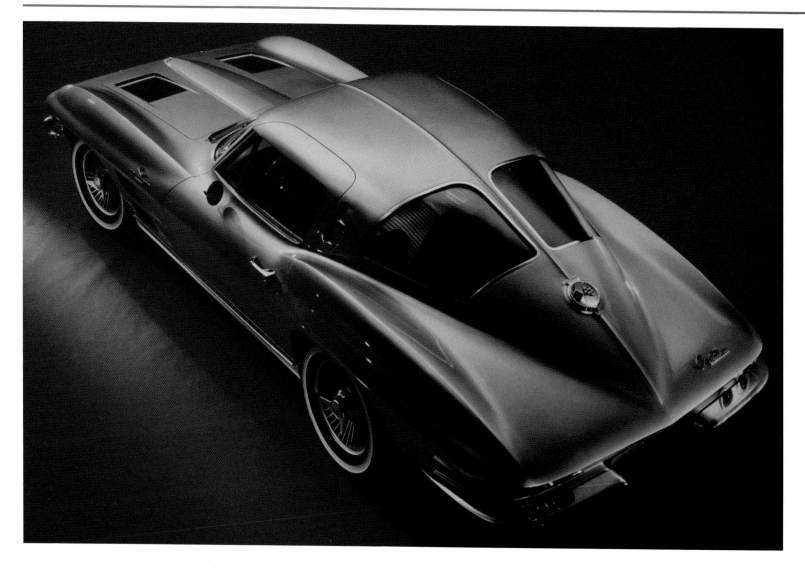

MODEL HISTORY

1953

Corvette launched.
Highlights include
Harley Earl-designed
fibreglass body, but a
very high sticker price

1958

Production almost
cancelled. Corvette
saved by Zora
Arkus-Duntov who
fits the first V8

1963

C2 Sting Ray launched
– for many the most
beautiful Corvette ever

1968

C3 launched, based on
Mako Shark II
concept car. T-top
introduced

1984

C4 goes on sale. The
hardest working
Corvette lasts 12 years

Cadillac or even an imported Jaguar.

For '54 Chevrolet offered a wider choice of colors (black, blue and red) and offered a beige interior option, but mechanically and visually the Corvette was unchanged. Sales picked up to more than 3,000, though.

But 1955 nearly saw the death of the Corvette. Sales plummeted to just 700 and the money men within GM wanted to axe the car. Salvation came in the form of a man named Zora Arkus-Duntov. As a former racing driver he believed what the car really needed was more power and better handling. So in went a 265 cubic inch V8 with 195bhp and an optional three-speed manual transmission. At Daytona Duntov ran the measured mile at 150mph and a legend was born.

Over the next two years the 'Vette really came into its own, A '56 restyle gave birth to the famous scalloped sides. In 1957 came a 283 cubic inch V8 offering 220bhp as standard, but with the 'Fuelie' motor a hefty 283bhp. Enough for the Corvette to crack the quarter mile in 14 seconds. Now the 'Vette was a major performance player.

Between '58 and '62 the styling evolved gradually and so did the speed. By the time the end of the line came for the mark one 'Vette a 327 cubic inch V8 was now standard and horsepower had shot up to 360bhp with the 'Fuelie' motor.

1963 brought the Sting Ray body in convertible or split window coupe styles. For many people this is the ultimate Corvette, and in Z06 race trim it was a major player. Over the four years of the second generation Corvette, handling was uprated, brakes became all-wheel discs and the engine choice was widened to include a number of 327 V8s and a mighty 427. Officially rated at 430bhp, true figures of up to 600bhp were widely talked about.

Based closely on GM's Mako Shark II concept the C3 'Vette made its debut in 1968. New features included a removable

1963 brought the new Sting Ray body. For many people this is the ultimate Corvette

1990
The ZR-1 is unveiled with 375bp – the most powerful Corvette since the 1970s

1996
C5 hits the road and the T-top returns

2001
Z06 offers 385bhp

2004
C6 arrives with 400bhp as standard

2005
Z06 is the fastest, most powerful Corvette ever, with 500bhp

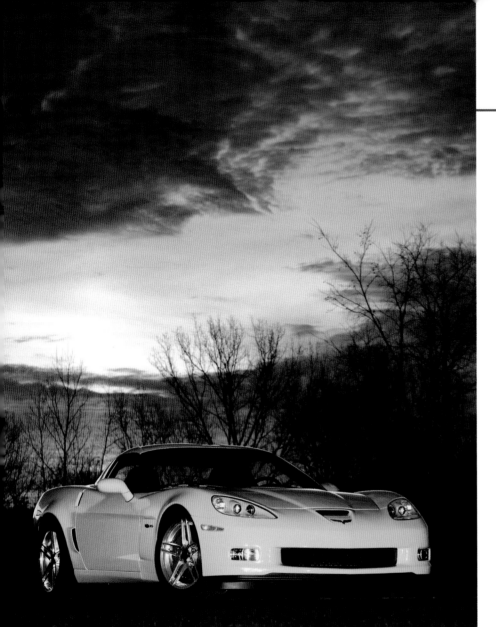

The C4 (below) was the longest-lived 'Vette. The 2003 C5 celebrated 50 glorious years

T-top for the Stingray coupe and a three-speed automatic gearbox to replace the old two-speed unit.

By 1970 the engine choice was a 350 V8 or a 450 although with 'only' 390bhp offered on the top flight LS5. A year later came the LS6 and power was back up to 430bhp again.

Throughout the Seventies the Corvette was progressively modernised, most notably with the introduction of Federal bumpers in 1974. And in a nod to the oil crisis, the big block V8 disappeared, with only the 350 remaining for the rest of this model's life. The Stingray name also disappeared.

The fourth generation 'Vette had the longest lifespan. Launched in 1984 (no 'Vettes were sold at all in 1983) it soldiered on for 12 years. The styling was all-new and, although a significant change from the C3, it was perhaps the least visually exciting model. The 350 V8 was carried over and a four-speed manual or four-speed automatic was offered. Probably the most significant

THE ULTIMATE CORVETTE

Born out of tremendous success in the American Le Mans race series the 2006 Z06 is the ultimate Corvette. Its 427 cubic inch V8 packs 500bhp which means this amazing car can hit zero to sixty in four seconds, hack the quarter mile in less than 12 seconds and top out at more than 190mph.

But there's more to it than just horsepower. The hardtop body is super rigid, the brakes feature 14-inch cross-drilled discs and there are 18-inch front and 19-inch wheels. The suspension is stiffer and lower than standard and the whole car is wider than a normal C6.

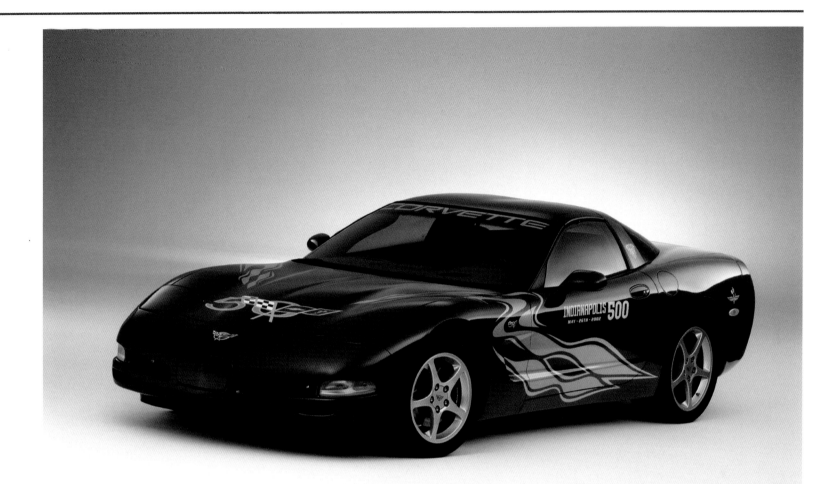

moment in the C4's life came in 1990 with the introduction of a six-speed manual gearbox and the launch of the ZR-1 with its mighty 375bhp. Three years later the ZR-1 was packing 405bhp, although it was only on sale for three years.

The C5 Corvette came along in '97 with a more compact and purposeful look, plus a new small block LS1 engine packing 345bhp. A convertible followed in '98 and a hard top in 1999. 2001 saw the return of the Z06 name with a 385bhp engine and uprated suspension, brakes, wheels and tires. A year later it was given another

20bhp to match the mighty ZR-1.

2003 marked the 50th anniversary of the 'Vette and to celebrate a limited run of cars was produced.

In 2004 the sixth generation Corvette hit the streets. Widely regarded as the most sophisticated and best-driving of the bunch, it comes with a six-litre (366 cubic inch) V8 offering 400bhp. Included were such high tech offerings as a Head Up Display, ABS brakes and Active Handling. In 2005 the Z06 returned with 500bp. America's Sports Car is now every bit the world player and able to rival the best of European exotica.

Specification

Years built	1953 to date
Most powerful model	2005 Z06
Engine type	V8
Displacement	427 cu in
Transmission	six-speed manual, rear-wheel drive
Power	500bhp
Top speed	190mph+

Sting Rays from 1963 (above) and 1965 (right)

1984 C4 (above) and 1968 T-top Stingray (left)

1996 C4 convert-
ible (above) and
1973 Stingray
hardtop,

2002 C5 (above) and 2005 C6 (left)

Chevrolet El Camino

The crazy El Camino brought muscle car madness to the pickup market

Chevrolet first introduced its oddball car/truck hybrid in 1959. Based on the Impala, it hardly set any sales records and only lasted two years.

It didn't take long for the name to reappear, though. In 1964 the El Camino was back. Now based on the Chevrolet Chevelle, the El Camino, meant business. Uner the hood came a choice of 283 or 327 cubic inch V8s. Power outputs were respectable, if not awe-inspiring, with the base car offering 195bhp and the top of the line packing 250bhp.

For real muscle El Camino fans would have to wait until 1968 for the arrival of the SS. By now the El Camino looked less truck-like than ever. It was long, low and lean, with its bonnet scoops emphasizing its performance potential.

Like its sister car the Chevelle SS this was a seriously powerful machine, driven by a 396 cubic inch V8 and available in three states of tune. There was 325bhp from the standard SS396, 350bhp from the L34 version and a heavyweight 375bhp from the L78. Given that this machine was essentially designed for the brick yard and not the Brickyard that was pretty impressive.

1970 saw the El Camino receive the same facelift as the Chevelle, and that brought even more power. Gone was the 396 engine to be replaced by a 300bhp 350 for the standard unit with a new 402 offering 350 or 375bhp. Not bad. Until you consider the 454 LS6 option that took the El Camino up to an astonishing 450bhp.

Now here was a pickup that could run the quarter mile in less than 14 seconds.

MODEL HISTORY

1959
El Camino first appears, based on the Impala

1964
After a short break it's back and now based on the Chevelle

1968
El Camino SS unveiled with 396 power

1970
The Ultimate El Camino arrives with an astonishing 450bhp.

1983
The final El Camino is built

Muscle car madness was at its height and the El Camino is probably the most bizarre example of the extreme lenths that car makers went to.

But just as the impending oil crisis and strict new emission rules hit the Chevelle SS, so they hit the El Camino and in 1971 it was massively detuned. Even the LS6 was down to just 365bhp; less than the L78 of 1969. It marked the beginning of the end.

A year later and the most powerful El Camino produced just 270bhp and by the time the final incarnation came along – based now on the Chevy Malibu – there was a maximum of just 245bhp on offer.

The El Camino continued in production until 1983, but never again reached the great heights of 1970.

Its glory days may have been quite short but the Chevrolet El Camino will always be remembered as one of the most unique machines of the muscle era.

Specification

Years built	1959 to 1973
Most powerful model	1970 SS
Engine type	V8
Displacement	454 cu in
Transmission	Turbo-Hydramatic
Power	450bhp
Top speed	130mph

This was a pickup that could run the quarter-mile in 14 secs. Muscle car madness was at its height

Chevrolet Impala SS

The Impala could just be the car that started muscle car mania

Several cars claim credit for spawning the muscle car craze and Chevrolet's Impala is no exception. Born in 1958 as the highest specification Bel Air, the Impala was Chevrolet's most expensive model. It came as a hardtop or convertible with no less than seven engine options varying from just 145bhp to 315bhp.

A year later the Impala was a stand-alone model. It was longer, wider and only a Cadillac offered more outrageous Batmobile styling. Over the next two years the styling was tamed, but 1961 would be a memorable year thanks to the introduction of the Impala Super Sport or SS. By now the Impala was available with a choice of three 348 cid V8s with 305, 340 or 350bhp plus a mighty 409 offering 360bhp.

In 1962 a pair of four-barrel carbs was added to the huge 409 engine, giving the Impala one horsepower for every cubic inch. By 1963 they had raised the ante again and the Impala packed 430bhp with a special Z-11 427 cubic inch lump.

MODEL HISTORY

1958

Impala introduced as top of the line Bel Air

1961

Super Sport option goes on sale. Epic 409 engine is most powerful

1969

Impala reaches the end of the road

1994

Impala returns for two years as a rebadged Chevy Caprice

2004

Impala returns again – with front wheel drive!

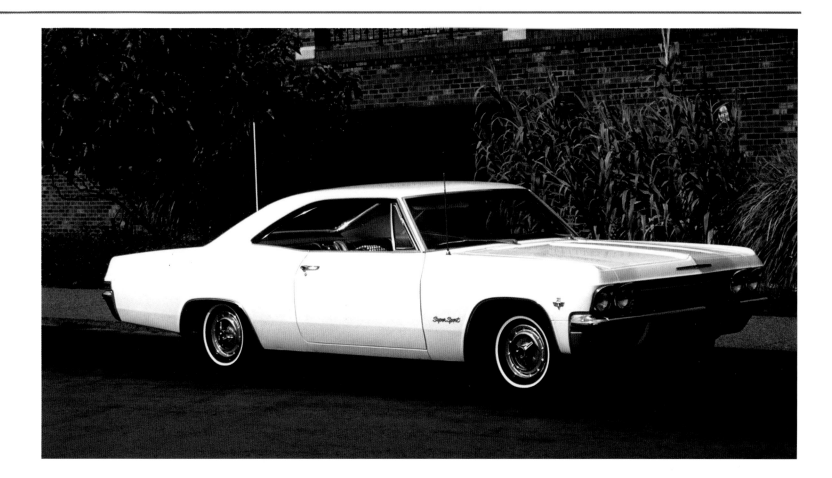

1965 saw a total overhaul of the design, with a more streamlined look. Out went the 409 engine and in came a new 396. A year later the Impala was no longer King of the Hill at Chevrolet due to the arrival of the Caprice and both sales and the car's prestige gradually went into to decline. The last Impala of this generation rolled off the production line in 1969.

Chevrolet briefly revived the Impala SS name from 1994 to 1996 when it wanted to add some spice to the Caprice range. A 350 V8 offered 260bhp, but it was a large and staid-looking machine, and despite a reasonable turn of speed, it wasn't really worthy of the badge.

The Impala reappeared once more in 2000, but now with front-wheel drive and even the latest 2005 SS with its 240bhp supercharged V6 engine can hardly be mentioned in the same breath as the original. The Impala's muscle car days are long gone.

Specification

Years built	1958 to date
Most powerful model	1963 SS
Engine type	V8
Displacement	409 cu in
Transmission	four-speed manual
Power	430bhp
Top speed	130mph

1961 would be a memorable year thanks to the introduction of the Impala Super Sport

Chrysler 300

Chrysler's luxury 300 started Detroit's horsepower race in 1955 and launched the epic Hemi engine

If one car can take responsibility for the start of Detroit's horsepower race, it's the Chrysler 300. This luxurious coupe, launched in 1955 came with a 331 cubic inch V8 engine as standard. And it was no ordinary V8, either. It was the first Hemi.

Named after the hemispherical shape of the combustion chambers it produced 300bhp. Mated to a PowerFlite transmission, the C-300 burnt its special Blue Streak racing tyres when it ran the flying mile at 127.58mph. This first Chrysler 'letter car' was not cheap, though. And only 1,725 were built.

A year later the 300B was released. Power now came from a 354 cid Hemi with 340bhp as standard or 355bhp in high output form. Once again the 300 set the world alight by achieving close to 140mph in the flying mile.

In 1957 the Hemi packed even more

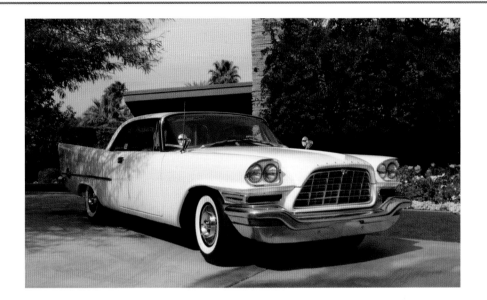

At Bonneville Salt
Flats a 300D set a
new speed record of
156.387mph

*1955 original (opposite page),
1958 (above) and
2005 (right)*

power. With a 392 cid capacity it had 375bhp as standard, but if that wasn't enough then a high output version came with 390bhp thanks to a more extreme cam and bigger exhausts. Mated to a four-speed manual transmission the 300B could run the quarter-mile in 17 seconds and crack zero to sixty in just 7.7 seconds. Available as a two-door hardtop or convertible the 300 was establishing a reputation as a real high performance machine.

For '58 the car was renamed 300D and once more Hemi power was raised. Now 380bhp was standard and 390bhp came with the optional addition of electronic fuel injection. Unfortunately the innovative system wasn't very reliable and few buyers opted for it. At Bonneville Salt Flats a 300D set a new speed record of 156.387mph.

In '59 the Hemi was replaced by a new Golden Lion 413 cid V8 with 380bhp

In 2004 Chrysler unveiled a new 300. And, just like the original, it packs a Hemi

and a year later a 400bhbp version of the same engine was offered.

1961's 300G was completely restyled and the number of luxury options increased to include a six-way power seat and power door locks amongst a multitude of gadgets.

By the close of 1963 the Chrysler 300 was no more, but the final incarnation, the 300J was the fastest of them all (in standard production form). A new, more aerodynamic body helped it to 142mph.

And that was it for 40 years. But in 2004 Chrysler unveiled a new 300. And, just like the original, it packs Hemi power. Voted 2005 Car of the Year by Motor Trend, the

new 300 comes only as a four-door. But its low roofline and ground-hugging stance give it the look of a coupe.

There's a 3.5-liter (213 cid) V6 as standard, but it's the two Hemi engines that have got enthusiasts raving about the 300 again. As standard the 5.7-liter (348 cid) Hemi offers 340bhp, and in 6.1-liter (372 cid) SRT-8 trim there's 425bhp – more even than the greatest 300 of the 1960s muscle car heyday.

The 300 is rear-drive and comes with a five-speed Autostick transmission giving a choice of fully automated or manual shifts. Loaded with electronic driver aids and a taut chassis the 300 handles corners just as well as the straights. And it's every bit as luxurious as a 300 should be.

The name Chrysler 300 name evokes some emotive memories, and it looks set to create some new ones, too.

Specification

Years built	1955 to 1963, 2003 to date
Most powerful model	2005 SRT-8
Engine type	V8
Displacement	372 cu in
Transmission	five-speed automatic
Power	425bhp
Top speed	150mph

MODEL HISTORY

1955
Chrysler launches 300 with a 300bhp Hemi engine and starts the horsepower war

1956
300 achieves 140mph in the flying mile

1958
Electronic fuel injection offered as an option

1958
300D enters the record books with 156mph run at Bonneville Salt flats

1959
Hemi engine dropped in favour of Golden Lion V8

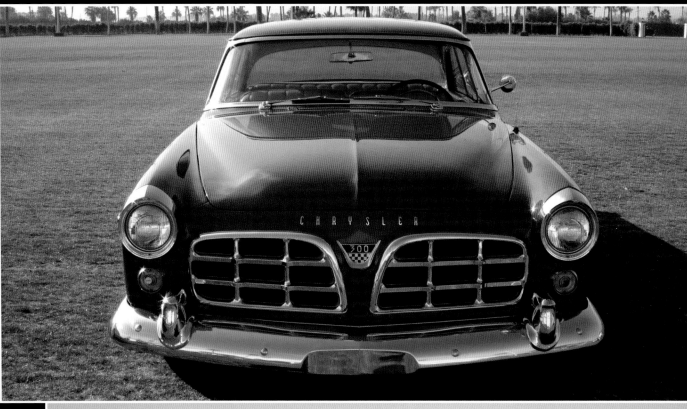

*1955 300 (above)
and meeting 2005
SRT-8 (right)*

2005 SRT-8 (above) and 1955 300-C (left)

Dodge Challenger

It was a late challenge by Dodge but this car certainly made a big impact

The Challenger joined the muscle car market pretty late, but despite a lifespan of only five years, it really made its mark on the scene.

What was so impressive about this Plymouth Barracuda-based model when it first went on sale in 1970 was the wide range of engines available.

Performance versions, badged R/T (Road/Track) came as standard with a 335bhp 383 cid engine, with two optional 440 cid V8s available: the four-barrel Magnum with 375bhp and the triple-carburated Six Pack with 390. Top dog was the awesome 426 Hemi with an outrageous 425bhp.

The 440s and Hemi came with TorqueFlite automatic transmission as standard , with a four-speed stick shift and limited slip differential both optional. Just to

give you even more choice, the Charger came in hardtop two-door or convertible body styles. It was some line-up.

Dodge even built a street version of its Trans Am racecar, the Challenger T/A, but when the company's lack of success on the race track caused them to pull out after the 1970 series, they pulled the plug on the road car as well.

The Challenger's late start meant that it hit 1971's new, stricter US emissions laws in only its second year, and sales dropped off along with the power output of the engines. The Hemi retained its 425bhp rating and was still offered, but the 440 Six Pack was now reduced to 385bhp.

The Challenger's reputation was tarnished even further when a bright orange convertible, acting as pace car for the Indy

MODEL HISTORY

1970
Challenger is launched with an impressive engine line-up including jaw-dropping 426 Hemi

1971
A Challenger pace car crashes into a press box at the Indy 500. The press are not impressed

1972
New grille fails to hid the fact that the Challenger is losing its muscle, with top power only 240bhp

1973
New 360 V8 only makes 5bhp more than the 340 that it replaces

1974
The Challenger bites the dust

500, crashed very publicly into the press box. Talk about bad publicity.

In 1972, the R/T performance version was discontinued and the convertible version that caused so much embarassment at Indianapolis in 1971 was also dropped. Coincidence?

By now a 340 cid V8 with just 240bhp was the biggest engine on offer. Symbolic of the Challenger's emasculation was the R/T's replacement, the new Rallye edition, which packed only a 318 cubic inch V8 with just 150bhp.

When even that was dropped in '73, the only option for those looking for any kind of performance became the new, 245bhp 360 engine – and it remained so until Dodge admitted that the Challenger

had been defeated in 1974.

The Challenger didn't stay long, but when a car quite literally makes such a big impact, it will never be forgotten.

Specification

Years built	1970 to 1975
Most powerful model	426 Hemi
Engine type	V8
Displacement	426 cu in
Transmission	TorqueFlite automatic
Power	425bhp
Top speed	140mph

The Challenger's reputation was further tarnished when a convertible crashed at the Indy 500

Dodge Charger

Dodge's Mustang rival was late to the party, but Hemi power made it a legend that lives on today

Dodge was caught short by the arrival of the Ford Mustang and the Plymouth Barracuda, but the car that it did finally bring to the muscle car party would be one of the most memorable of this great era.

The Dodge Charger was first shown to the public during the auto show season of 1965 as the Charger II concept car. It had a sleek two-door fastback body, hidden headlamps and full-width tail lamps. Inside were four bucket seats that further emphasized this car's performance potential. Within a year the production Charger was on sale, based on the Coronet, but looking almost identical to the show car, right down to those bucket seats.

Backing up that need for speed styling was a choice of V8 engines. Standard issue was a 318 cubic incher with 230bhp and next up was a 361 with 265bhp but the most popular choice would prove to be the 383

The Charger had the ability to run from zero to sixty in 6.4 seconds and do the quarter-mile in 14

1966 Original (opposite page) and concepts from 1965 (above)and 1999(right)

with its 335bhp giving owners plenty of bangs per buck.

The most spectacular, however, was the 426 Street Hemi. Race-bred, but tuned for the road, this legendary engine had an official rating of 425bhp, but it was a lie. The truth is that this amazing motor had closer to 500bhp. And that gave the Charger the ability to run from zero to sixty in 6.4 seconds and do the standing quarter-mile in just 14 seconds. But the Hemi was expensive, adding $1,000 to the price tag and although Chargers were leaving Dodge dealerships faster than they could build them, few were Hemis.

For 1967 Dodge found a cheaper alternative for those demanding serious horsepower. In went the 440 Magnum engine as part of the Charger's R/T pack. This was Chrysler's biggest engine and weighed in with 375bhp. It ran the Hemi

MUSCLE CARS

MODEL HISTORY

1965
Charger II concept car unveiled

1966
Charger hits the streets with awesome Hemi engine as an option

1967
440 Magnum engine offered

1968
First major restyle

1969
Charger 500 and Daytona launched. The year of the General Lee

close in performance, but real hardcore performance fans could still choose the 426.

1968 saw the Charger's first major restyle with a new grille hiding the headlights, and a tweaked tail. The so-called Scat Pack added bumble bee stripes.

The big news for '69 came from the racing scene, with the NASCAR-derived Charger 500 and Daytona hitting the road and track. The regular Charger was pretty much unchanged from '68. It's probably the most famous, though – thanks to a starring role as The General Lee in the hit TV show The Dukes of Hazzard. The General Lee not only charged, it frequently flew as well and during filming some 309 cars were used and most were wrecked, making any surviving '69 Chargers the most desirable.

1970 brought a second facelift that included a bold chrome loop front bumper and new tail lights. A new range of colors included Plum Crazy and Go-Mango, and the four-speed shifter now boasted a very cool pistol grip. In the engine bay there was a new option; the 440 Six Pack which ditched the standard four-barrel caburator in favour of three Holley two-barrel carbs. The result was rise from 375bhp to 390bhp.

The early '70s brought doom and gloom. The restyled 1971 Charger now shared its body with the Dodge Super Bee and power outputs dropped, although not as much as rival muscle cars. However, Chrysler couldn't hold out for long and 1971 saw the end of the Hemi.

1973 arrived with another restyle. Hidden headlights vanished from the options list and the styling was softened. The suspension was, too, meaning the Charger was no longer a real street racer.

For true fans the Charger died in 1974, the car that wore the Charger badge from 1975 to 1978 was little more than a renamed Chrysler Cordoba and was certainly no muscle car.

But for 2006 Chrysler is reviving the Charger name and the car's true spirit. It's

The 1969 Charger is probably the most famous thanks to the Dukes of Hazzard

THE ULTIMATE
CHARGER

Many will argue that a '68 Street Hemi should be king of the Chargers, but the fact is the latest 2006 SRT-8 would nail it in a straight line and around every corner. With its 425bhp Hemi engine it's got less raw power than a '68 but it weighs less too and is able to run from zero to sixty in five seconds and do the quarter-mile in 13 seconds. More impressively it can go from 0-100mph-0 in 16 seconds and stop from 60mph in just 110 feet. Special tuned SRT suspension is fitted alongside Brembo brakes and Goodyear F1 Supercar tires on 20-inch alloy wheels.

been a long time coming, with a sleek aerodynamic four-door concept car first being unveiled in 1999. Its teardop shape was wind-tunnel sculpted but somehow didn't seem aggressive enough to wear the legendary Charger badge.

2006's Charger is more muscular, with a blunt snout and kicked up flanks. The high sides and low glass area give the Charger an almost coupe-like look, despite it actually having four doors. Charger purists have bemoaned this decision and the fact that beneath the styling, the new Charger is essentially the same as the Chrysler 300C. But remember, the original Charger was based on the Coronet, so platform sharing has a long history within the Chrysler group.

No enthusiast will have any gripes about the Charger's powerplant. Budget buyers can opt for a 3.5-liter (214 cid) High Output V6 engine with 250 horsepower, but it's the revived Hemi that will get Charger fans going.

The 5.7-liter (347 cid) Hemi packs a

1999 concept car with ancestors (right), 2006 Charger Police spec (below)

340bhp punch and empowers the Charger with a zero to sixty time of just six seconds. Drive goes to the rear thanks to a five-speed automatic transmission with Chrysler's Autostick manual override system.

And as if that wasn't enough the SRT-8 version has an enlarged 6.1-liter (372 cid) Hemi with 425bhp – that's a power output right back to the good old days of the late 1960s.

But where the new Charger differs substantially is in its all-round performance ability. The original Charger would charge all right, but cornering and stopping weren't its favourite tasks. The 2006 Charger runs on 18-inch performance tires and tuned dampers and there's a Performance Handling Group option to give more steering feedback, better grip and enhanced road-holding. The SRT-8 also gets special Brembo brakes for added stopping power.

Maybe a '69 Hemi could just match the 2006 car in a straight line, but there's no way it could keep up in the corners.

The 2006 Charger may not be quite the same beast as the original, but times change, and the new Charger is every bit the 21st century muscle car.

Specification

Years built	1966 to 1978, 2005 to date
Most powerful model	2005 SRT-8
Engine type	V8
Displacement	372 cu in
Transmission	five-speed Autostick
Power	425bhp
Top speed	160mph

1969 Charger (above) and 1968 Charger III concept (right)

1968 model (above) and 1965 Charger II concept (left)

2006 SRT-8 (above) and 1999 Charger concept

2006 R/T Chargers (above) and 2006 SRT-8 (left)

Dodge Coronet

Packing a full race 426 Hemi V8, the Coronet was a mid-size with major muscle

Dodge had used, and then dropped, the Coronet name back in the Fifties, but it returned to grace its new midsize muscle car in 1965.

This car meant business right from the start, being available with the awe-inspiring full race 426 Hemi. This race-bred V8, seriously under-rated at 425bhp, was a little too uncivilised for most folks, though, and the following year saw the arrival of the Street Hemi. Made more manageable by the fitting of a hydraulic lifter cam and a lower compression ratio, it still made the Coronet a fearsomely high performance car.

New for 1967 was the Coronet R/T, marketed as the model equally at home on road or track. It came with heavy-duty suspension and the standard power unit was a new Magnum 440 cid V8, giving 375bhp when fitted with a four-barrel carburator and working through automatic or four-speed manual transmission. The

MODEL HISTORY

1965
Coronet instantly stamps its mark on the muscle car scene, with full race 426 Hemi

1966
The Street Hemi is introduced – same engine but a slightly less raw state of tune

1967
Coronet R/T arrives, with standard Magnum 440, and the range is facelifted

1968
Full restyle introduces more rounded lines, but Charger and Super Bee steal Coronet's thunder

1970
Another facelift, but this is the final year of the high performance Coronets

Coronet range also received a facelift which added such performance pointers as dummy air vents, racing stripes and deep front bucket seats.

A full restyle in 1968 resulted in more flowing, Coke-bottle-inspired lines, but internal competition from other Dodge performance models was looming. The R/T badging was now shared with the more expensive, more alluring Charger and midway through the year the company's new Super Bee undercut the Coronet on price.

The next year saw a new optional engine, the 440 Six Pack, created by fitting three two-barrel carbs to the existing 440 cid V8 and endowing it with 390bhp. The Hemi was still available, along with the original 440, but sales of the Coronet overall were on a definite downward trend.

A restyled front end in 1970 failed to attract further buyers and the R/T and convertible models were discontinued. From 1971 on, the Coronet was only available as a four-door sedan or station wagon and its days as a muscle car were over.

Specification

Years built	1965 to 1970
Most powerful model	1965 426 Hemi
Engine type	V8
Displacement	426 cu in
Transmission	four-speed manual
Power	425bhp
Top speed	130mph

This car meant business right from the start, being available with the awe-inspiring full race 426 Hemi

Dodge Daytona

Dodge's monster racecar for the road was the talk of 1969

Outrageous. That's the only way to describe the Dodge Daytona. Its eye-popping looks and jaw-dropping performance were borne of the company's desire to win races in the hotly-contested NASCAR series.

In 1969, the science of aerodynamics was at the cutting edge of race development, with the slippery shapes of Ford's Torino Talladega and Mercury Cyclone Spoiler gaining supremacy. But Dodge's engineers knew they could do better – and created a wild, 18-foot long supercar in the process.

They took the existing Charger 500 into surgery, adding a wedged nosecone and a massive spoiler at the rear. The Daytona emerged from the wind tunnel with a drag coefficient of just 0.28 (compare that to the modern Dodge Viper's figure of 0.5!).

There would have been even less drag if it weren't for that huge rear wing, which helped to maintain traction on the rear at high speed. And what a high speed! A Daytona racecar hit the headlines with a world closed-course speed record of

MODEL HISTORY

1969

Dodge Charger 500 racecar receives heavy aerodynamic restyle and the Daytona is born

1969

The company has to sell 500 road cars for the racecar to become eligible for NASCAR

1969

The car takes the first four places at Daytona, fulfilling Dodge's racing ambitions

1969

Sales of the street car fail to follow on from the racing success, with only 503 produced

1970

The Daytona doesn't make it into Dodge's road car brochure

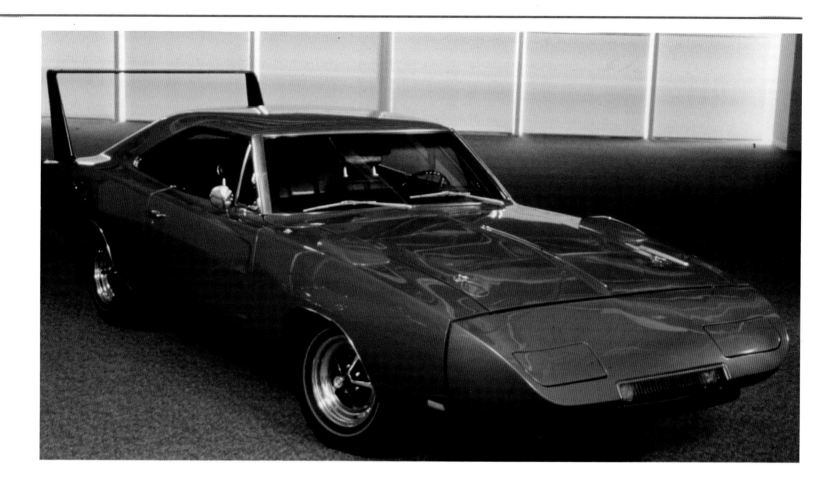

201.14mph and another reached 217mph at the Bonneville salt flats.

For the racecar to be eligible for NASCAR, Dodge had to sell 500 Daytonas to the public, so the guy on the street had the chance to buy a hardcore track car that was road legal. The $4,000 price tag was high but not exorbitant, with the standard 440-engined version offering a cheaper option and, with 375bhp, more than enough power for most people. The fearsome 426 Hemi, with its race-bred 425bhp V8, was not for the faint-hearted.

But although the Daytona proved a success on the track, the road car only racked up 503 sales and didn't make it to Dodge's 1970 model roster. The very thing that made it a winner on the track – its aerodynamic add-ons – proved a turn-off for the public. And so did its habit of overheating at speeds below 55mph – a problem that was solved, to greater sales success, by the next year's Plymouth Superbird.

Specification

Years built	1969
Most powerful model	1969 426 Hemi
Engine type	V8
Displacement	426 cu in
Transmission	four-speed manual
Power	425bhp
Top speed	160mph

A Daytona racecar hit the headlines with a world closed-course speed record of 201.14mph

Dodge
Super Bee

Dodge's answer to the Plymouth Road Runner never quite took off

The late Sixties saw the height of performance mania in the USA, and with the effects of prosperity filtering down to the country's youth, virtually every 20-year-old with a job could afford an automobile.

This was an emerging market that astute car manufacturers were keen to tap into, with Plymouth launching its budget-priced performance car, the Road Runner, in 1968. That spurred Dodge, Plymouth's fellow Chrysler brand, to bring out its own vehicle for giving the kids cheap thrills – the Super Bee.

Released to the public later that same year, the Dodge also shared the same basic chassis, had a virtually identical curb weight, and was offered with the same range of engines as the Plymouth. But the Road Runner undercut the Super Bee's $3,027 base price by $131, putting the Dodge at a disadvantage from day one.

Still, at least the Super Bee looked the part. Bold bumble bee stripes circled the car's tail and it wore a big Super Bee emblem proudly on its flanks. The grille was a sinister matte black and the hood was adorned with aggressive air scoops.

Based on the redesigned Coronet pillared coupe, the Super Bee was offered with only two engines: the standard 335bhp 383 cubic inch V8 or the Chrysler group's prodigiously powerful 426 Hemi.

It may seem strange today, with original Hemi Super Bees hitting prices near to $100,000, but as this engine option added $1,000 to the price, the car's budget-conscious buyers tended to shy away from it.

The Bee's low purchase price was

MODEL HISTORY

1968
Super Bee introduced as a rival to Plymouth's successful Road Runner

1969
Two-door hardtop model joins the original pillared coupe

1970
A restyle and a $64 drop in price fail to stop sales dropping

1970
Wild colors like Plum Crazy and Go-Mango are offered

1971
Super Bee adopts Dodge Charger platform, but the buzz is over

achieved by minimising equipment. Automatic transmission was an option from the standard four-speed manual shift, but if you wanted disc brakes, air conditioning or cruise control, the 1969 Dodge Super Bee couldn't deliver.

The same year saw the arrival of the Six Pack engine, as offered in the rest of Dodge's muscle car roster, giving buyers an optional 390bhp powerplant topped off with a wild, air-scooped hood. Made of fiber glass it even had NASCAR-style tie-downs to complete the street racer look.

Although a capable budget muscle car, the Super Bee was overshadowed by the cooler image and greater sales success of its in-house rival, the Road Runner.

Despite 1970's eye-popping color schemes (such as Plum Crazy and Go-Mango) and a switch to the Dodge Charger platform in 1971, the model didn't make it into the 1972 sales season.

Specification

Years built	1968 to 1971
Most powerful model	1968 426 Hemi
Engine type	V8
Displacement	426 cu in
Transmission	Four-speed manual
Power	425bhp
Top speed	125mph

Bumble bee stripes circled the car's tail and it wore a big Super Bee emblem proudly on its flanks

Dodge Viper

The Viper was a concept car made real and it turned round Dodge's fortunes in the 1990s

The Dodge Viper exploded onto the scene at the 1989 Detroit Auto Show and moved the muscle car into a whole new era. Big, brash and brawny, this concept car seemed way too extreme for a company like Chrysler to put into production. But, within three years the Viper was in the showrooms and an American dream was realized.

But it was harsh reality that helped create this dream car, which spearheaded an attempt by Chrysler to re-energize itself. The corporation was struggling in the late Eighties and its Vice President, car nut Bob Lutz, was looking to produce a headline-grabbing sports car to put it back on the map. When Carroll Shelby, the famous Texan ex-racer and creator of the legendary AC Cobra of the Sixties, joined the project, he brought with him a burning desire to reproduce his success in building an iconic American performance car.

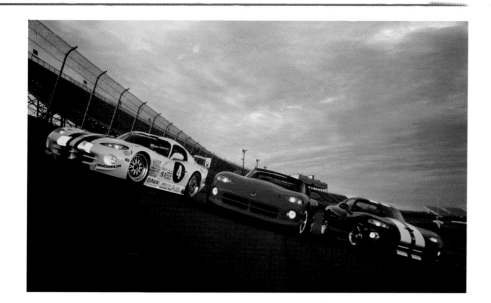

Big, brash and brawny, this concept car seemed way too extreme for a company like Chrysler

2003 SRT-10 (left), first gen trio (above), 1989 concept (right)

That was exactly what ended up wowing the crowds at that Detroit Show – the spiritual descendant of the awesome Cobra. A raw, no-frills beast with monstrous power from a huge V10 engine, the Viper's vital statistics were: 488 cubic inches displacement, 400 horsepower and 465 lbft of torque, figures to whet the appetite of any red-blooded sports car fan. The bodywork was pure muscle, a strict two-seater layout fleshed out with beefy haunches and a huge hood to cover that aluminum-block V10 which promised 160mph performance. By the time the first Vipers rolled out of the showrooms, it was 1992, and Dodge's first true sports car for years attacked its task of returning the company to its former glories with venom. As celebrity owners such as Jay Leno snapped them up, Chrysler was suddenly cool again.

Nothing could challenge the Viper's

MODEL HISTORY

1989

The Viper concept car makes its first public appearance, wowing the Detroit Auto Show

1989

A wave of positive feedback convinces Chrysler bosses to put it into production

1992

First R/T model cars are delivered to buyers. Only 285 are made – all in red

1996

GTS fixed-head coupe version launched with an uprated 450bhp engine

1996

RT/10 upped to 415bhp when side-exit exhausts are replaced by a rear-exit system reign as the supreme expression of American automobile performance, and it remained basically unrivalled for nearly a decade. The introduction of the GTS coupe in 1996 provided a hardtop alternative to the R/T model's removable roof and featured an uprated 450bhp engine, but changed little else. The Viper was continuing to prove a popular image-booster but it needed an overhaul to maintain its profile.

When Dodge engineers literally tried to change the car's profile by adding a few inches to the wheelbase, they discovered that they would also need to rework most of the body panels and suspension. So they decided they may as well create an entirely new car: a true convertible with a revised chassis and shell... and an even bigger, more powerful engine!

Dodge realized the passion that the Viper stirred in its owners, so what better way to gauge what the next-generation car should be like than to ask them? The feedback from current owners of the car was resounding: they wanted more power, less weight, bigger brakes and no unnecessary add-ons like cruise control or cupholders. In a true power-to-the-people gesture, Dodge set to its task...

When the new 2003 Viper SRT-10 emerged, it performed pretty much to the brief these owners had given. For starters, it was 100 pounds lighter than the outgoing model. The car still packed a V10 under the hood, but the new engine displaced 505 cubic inches, producing 500 horsepower and a massive 525 lbft of torque. The

previous model's six-speed manual transmission was beefed up to take the extra punishment. A stiffer chassis held everything together, with revised suspension devised to tame some of the Viper's unpredictable behaviour when driven in anger – this new snake would be less willing to bite its driver.

The new suspension also improved ride quality and the brakes received the prescribed attention too, with improved

> Nothing could challenge the Viper's reign as the supreme expression of American performance

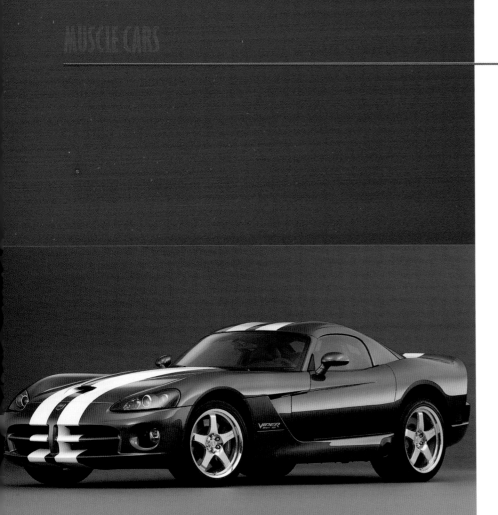

Brembo calipers which Dodge claimed would haul the car to a stop from 60mph in an impressive 100 feet. And the remainder of the SRT-10's performance statisics are equally staggering: 0-60mph in less than four seconds, a top speed of 190mph and 0-100-0mph in less than 13 seconds. The Viper re-established its reputation as the wildest beast in the American auto world with a vengeance.

And the story didn't end there. The SRT-10's colossal rear wheels were the widest available on a stock US production car, at 19x13 inches – and the fronts were no slouches at 18x10. The huge contact area of the tires combined with the car's longer wheelbase made the big snake less unpredictable when really pushed.

The general refinements in the Viper's driving experience were echoed with appointments which made living with a Viper a little less rough and ready. The car was now a true convertible, doing away with the R/T's clumsy removable roof and replacing it with an easily-operated bi-fold

Latest SRT-10 on the road (below and right)

THE ULTIMATE
VIPER

The snake car continues to evolve, and the next expression of the Viper's extreme performance philosophy is the 2006 SRT-10 Coupe. The ultimate Viper, this car is based on the SRT-10 convertible, but with a fixed metal roof featuring 'double bubble' bulges to give more headroom for driver and passenger. That's to allow the wearing of crash helmets – so there's absolutely no doubt about this car's sporting intent! The 2006 Coupe's engine and drivetrain are shared with the convertible, so there's still 505 cubic inches of displacement, 500 horsepower and 525 lb-ft of torque driving through a six-speed manual transmission. But as the coupe is more aerodynamic than the convertible, it will beat the latter's 190mph top speed.

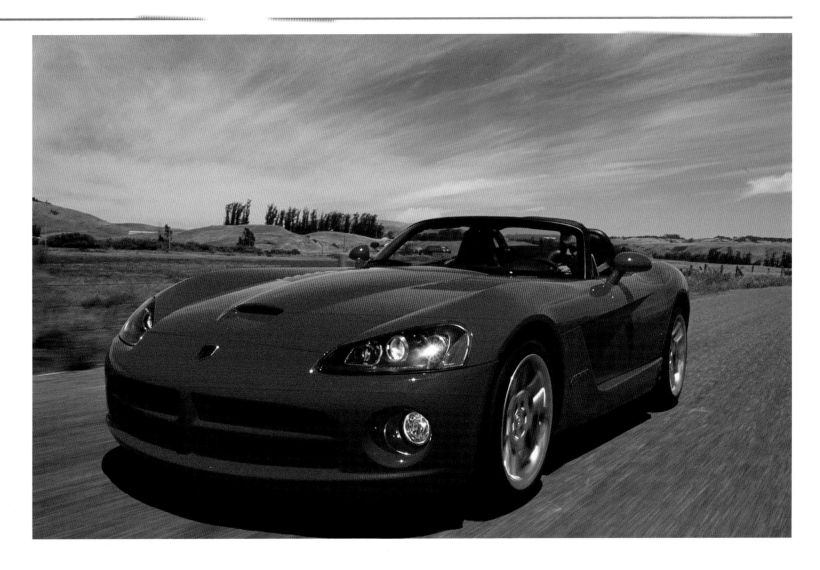

clamshell top which stowed neatly under the trunk lid. The new model also received a serious cabin makeover, banishing the old interior, with its creaky plastics and toy-like gauges, to the garbage can. Now the Viper owner could really enjoy a quality cockpit, rather than have to put up with a low-rent effort. And no, there were no cupholders...

Although still recognizably a Viper, the new model's bodywork was sleeker if a little less muscular than its predecessor. The new conventionally-hinged hood was certainly easier to handle than the old front-hinged job, which really required two people to open without a struggle. But you can't please all the people all the time, and some Viper fans mourned the passing of the 'cartoon muscle car' looks of the original.

Now well into its second decade, the Viper continues to provide the glamour that it first injected into the company back in 1992. Its reliability and longevity has been backed up by repeated success in endurance racing when pitched against the best the world can offer.

The Dodge Viper entered the public consciousness as a symbol of American muscle. With the SRT-10, the legend lives on.

Specification

Years built	1992 to date
Most powerful model	2005 SRT-10
Engine type	V10
Displacement	505 cu in
Transmission	six-speed manual, rear-wheel drive
Power	500bhp
Top speed	190mph

1997 R/T-10 (above) and an early '92 (right)

2003 SRT-10 (above) and early R/T-10 (left)

2003 SRT-10
(above) and
alongside 2006
Coupe (right)

2006 Coupe (above) and the concept that spawned it (left)

Ford Fairlane & Torino

The Fairlane was a real innovator, but it also had plenty of muscle. And as a Gran Torino it became one of the most popular TV cars ever

Probably one of the few cars to be named after a house – Henry Ford's Fair Lane mansion in Dearborn – the first Fairlanes in 1955 were not a lot faster. But over the next 16 years, this fairly ordinary family sedan evolved into a range of remarkable autos.

The 1957 'Skyliner' had the world's first fully retractable electrically-powered steel roof. The sleek 1960 'Starliner', a pillarless two-door hardtop, set the much-copied 'fastback' look. The 1962 Fairlane 500 Sports Coupe had bucket seats and an innovative lightweight thin-wall cast V8. The 1964 427 cubic inch Fairlane 'Thunderbolt' or 'T-Bolt', built specially for serious drag-strip racing, boasted a highly tuned 427 cubic inch V8 with an astonishing 500 bhp. Fairlane spin-offs, included the mighty Galaxie, the Fairlane GT and GTA, the 500 XL GT hardtop and convertible – and the most famous Fairlane of all, 'Zebra

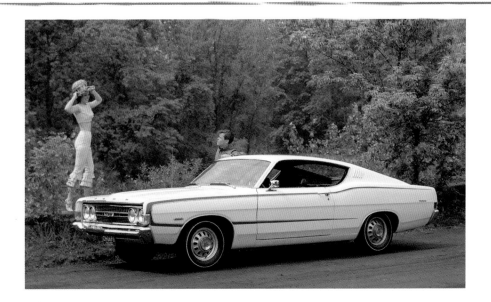

The most muscular
Fairlane ever has to be
the Thunderbolt rated
at 425bhp but actually
producing 500

*1967 Fairlane (opposite
page), 1969 Torino (above)
and 1969 convertible (right)*

Three' the red and white Gran Torino furiously driven by TV cops Starsky and Hutch from 1975 to 1979.

The Fairlane didn't enter the ranks of the muscle cars until the middle of 1962. The Fairlane 500 Sports Coupe was nearly a foot shorter than the previous year's car and boasted a new lightweight 'thin-wall-cast' 221 cubic inch V8. It even had European sports car style bucket seats.

The most muscular Fairlane ever has to be the 1964 Thunderbolt or 'T-Bolt'. Specially built for drag strip racing, the cars' big 427 cubic inch V8s were rated at 425 horsepower, but actually produced 500. In the 1964 NHRA's World Championship, a T-Bolt driven by Gas Ronda took 1st place, running the quarter-mile in 11.6 seconds with a terminal speed of 124 miles an hour. Just 111 T-Bolts were built.

In 1966 Ford added the Fairlane GT

The car became
so popular it
actually attracted
its own fan mail

and GTA 500 XL cars. These were fitted with Ford's big-block FE V8 and had special badges, body stripes, heavy duty suspension, disc brakes, bucket seats, and sports steering wheel. The XL featured a 390 cubic inch 335 horsepower V8 with a high-lift cam, performance manifolds and a four-barrel carb. To improve its muscle-car image Ford also made around 60 Fairlanes fitted with the famous 'side-oiler' 427 wedge engines that were raced in NASCAR. Two versions were offered with either 410 or 425bhp. The 425bhp car got to 60 miles an hour in six seconds and ran the quarter-mile in a respectable 14.5 seconds.

1968 saw the introduction of what would become the most famous Fairlane of all, the Torino. The most powerful version of that year boasted a 390bhp 427 cubic inch V8. In 1969 the Torino Cobra was added. With lowered and toughened suspension, wide wheels, black grille and hood air-scoop it looked the business and its 428 cubic inch Cobra Jet V8 was rated at 335bhp, but it really cranked out 400.

1975 was the year of the Torino, for the fall of 1975 saw the screening of the TV cop series Starsky and Hutch. Stars David Soul and Paul Michael Glaser thundered around in a red and white Gran Torino call-signed 'Zebra Three'. The car became so popular it actually attracted fan-mail, and Ford reacted by making 1,000 look-alikes. The TV car had a 400 cid V8, but the look-alike autos had a 351 cid V8, and with just 138bhp could hardly be called muscle cars.

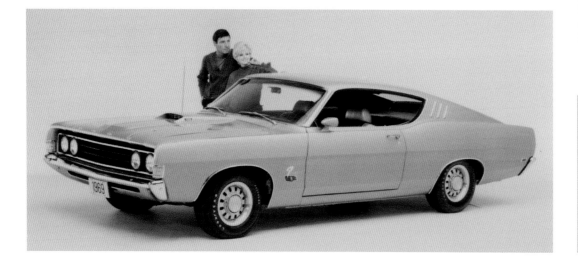

Specification

Years built	1955 to 1971
Most powerful model	1969 Fairlane Cobra
Engine type	V8
Displacement	428 cu in
Transmission	four-speed manual
Power	335bhp
Top speed	125mph

MODEL HISTORY

1955
Ford Fairlane launched as a top of the line full-size Ford in six different body styles

1957
Fairlane 500 Skyliner is the first in the world with an electric retractable hardtop

1960
The Fairlane 'Starliner', a pillarless two-door hardtop, set the much-copied 'fastback' look

1962
First of the Fairlane muscle-cars. Fairlane 500 Sports Coupe

1964
Thunderbolt drag-strip racer is most powerful version of the Fairlane with up to 500bhp

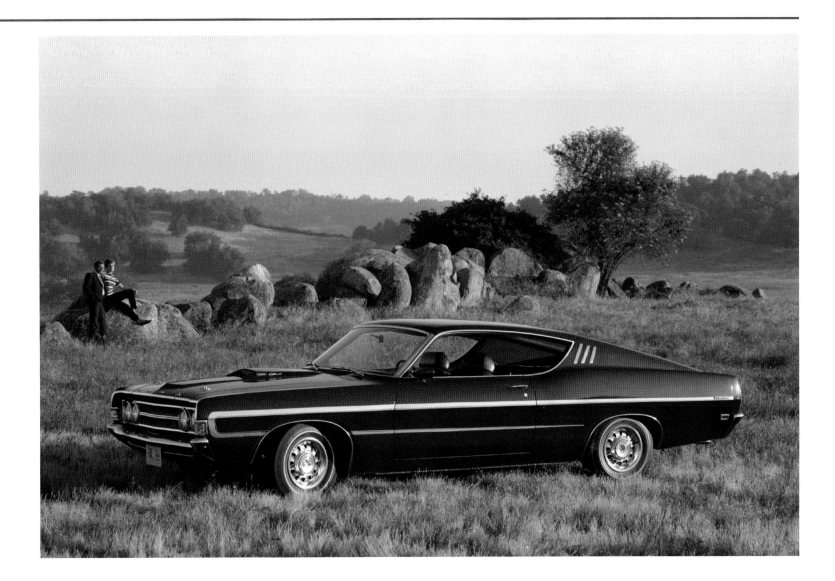

1966

60 Fairlane
500s and 500XLs built
with NASCAR 427 410
or 425 horsepower
'wedge' engines

1968

Fairlane Torino
launched with 390
horsepower 427 cubic
inch V8

1969

Fairlane Torino Cobra
added to range.
Aggressive looks
teamed with 400
horsepower

1970

Just one muscle-car left
in the range – the light-
weight Falcon offered
with the Boss 375
horsepower 429 V8

1975

Gran Torino stars in 92
episode cop series Starsky
and Hutch. Ford builds
1,000 look-alike red and
white 'Zebra Threes'.

Ford Galaxie

It was the most powerful muscle car ever made, but the Galaxie's performance didn't translate into sales

The Galaxie has the distinction of having the most powerful engine of the muscle-car era. The Cammer 427 engine was developed for the 1965 car and in its dual-four-barrel carb form was rated at a colossal 675bhp. It was, and probably still is, the most powerful production engine ever made in Detroit. However, it made the Galaxie almost impossible to drive on the street. Too few cars were fitted with it for NASCAR to accept the Cammer as a production engine and Ford reluctantly stopped production. But its reputation stands.

The first Galaxie was launched in 1959. It was big. It was heavy. It was wide. It also came with Ford's first production muscle-car engine, the 352 Interceptor Special V8. Rated at 360bhp, it had a four-barrel carb, 10.6:1 compression, a solid-lifter cam and a dual-point distributor.

In 1960 Ford withdrew from the Auto

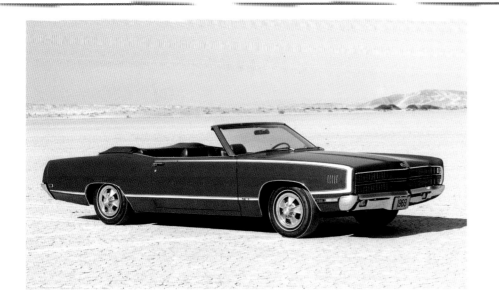

Rated at a colossal 675bhp it was, and probably still is, the most powerful engine ever made in Detroit

1969 convertible (above) and 1969 XL (opposite page and right)

Manufacturers Association's four year ban on stock car racing and almost immediately turned up at the Daytona Speedway with a 360bhp Galaxie Starliner that did 40 laps at an average speed of 142mph. The 1961 Starliner was smaller in size but much bigger-engined. In the middle of the year the 390 cubic inch V8 was available with a triple two-barrel carb rated at a massive 401 horsepower. It pushed the heavy Galaxie to 60 miles an hour in just seven seconds.

Cubic inches counted in the early 60s and Ford came up with the 406 cubic inch V8. With a single four-barrel Holly carb it was rated at 385bhp, and with three Holley dual-barrel carbs it put out 405bhp. Even then it was down four horses on Chevrolet's 409bhp 409 cubic inch V8. The 406 engine was a must to get the big and heavy Galaxies moving in a respectable fashion.

In 1962 the 406 engine was made

It won no

less than 23

Grand National

NASCAR races

available in the lighter Galaxie 500 and 500 XL. The XL had bucket seats and a center console. Both of these 'sportier' Galaxies came with floor-stick four-speed manual transmission, 15-inch instead of 14-inch wheels and heavy-duty suspension.

1963 turned out to be a good year for the Galaxie. The two-door hardtop was re-styled and lowered to improve aerodynamics, and with the new 427 cubic inch 425bhp motor, it won no less than 23 Grand National NASCAR races – including the top five places at Daytona.

Ford also built 50 lightweight Sports Roof Galaxies specially for competition.

And with the 425bhp 427 engine the light-weights could manage the quarter-mile in a respectable 12.07 seconds.

1965 saw the sensational Cammer 427, the most powerful production engine ever made in Detroit. With a single barrel carb, this twin-overhead camshaft was rated at a colossal 616bhp. With dual four-barrel carbs the power output was a hardly believable 675bhp. The 'cammer' Galaxie was impossible to drive on the street and NASCAR didn't accept it as too few were built. Neverless it did wonders for the Galaxie's reputation.

Unfortunately reputation didn't result in additional Galaxie sales and only 237 427-engined cars were sold in 1966. This signalled the end of the Galaxie's heydays as a muscle car. From 1967 until its demise in 1972, the Galaxie was developed and promoted as a large and luxurious limo.

Specification

Years built	1969 to 1972
Most powerful model	1965 Cammer
Engine type	V8
Displacement	427 cu in
Transmission	four-speed manual
Power	675bhp
Top speed	130mph

MODEL HISTORY

1959

Galaxie launched with Ford's first production muscle-car engine, the 352 Interceptor Special

1960

Galaxie Starliner does 40 laps at Daytona at an average speed of 142mph

1961

406 cubic inch V8 introduced. With three Holley dual-barrel carbs it puts out 405bhp

1962

Galaxie 500 and 500 XL introduced. Both come with floor-stick four-speed manual transmission

1963

Galaxie wins 23 Grand National NASCAR races – including the top five places at Daytona

1964

Lightweight Sports
Roof Galaxies run the
quarter-mile in
12.07 seconds

1965

Introduction of
Detroit's most powerful
production engine ever
– the 675bhp Cammer

1966

427-engined Galaxie
sales drop away with
just 237 cars sold

1987

Galaxie muscle car
image dropped as car is
promoted as luxury
limousine

1972

Galaxie production
ends. Top of the line
limo is the spacious
LTD Brougham

Ford GT

*To celebrate its 100th anniversary
Ford recreated a racing legend
with the glorious GT*

The tale of Ford's amazing GT40 has passed into automobile mythology. It's the story of an American company's burning desire to win the world's toughest endurance race against all the odds – a true story of guts and glory. This is a saga of such evocative power that its reprise, four decades after the original events, has led to the rebirth of a legend in the form of the awesome Ford GT.

The story begins back in the early Sixties, when Ford set itself the task of wining the prestigious Le Mans 24 Hour race. By taking the honours in this ultimate test of stamina the corporation hoped to increase sales of its road cars.

In an attempt to fast-track his company to sporting glory, Ford boss Henry Ford II tried to buy Ferrari, the Italian company which had made Le Mans its own with six consecutive victories. Rebuffed by the firm's owner, Enzo Ferrari, Ford

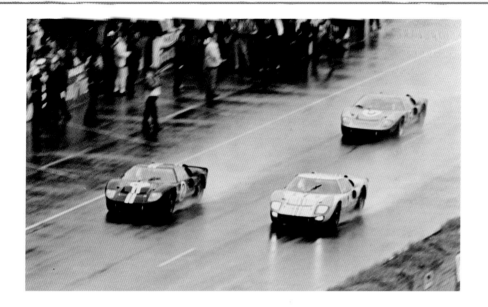

The tale of Ford's amazing GT40 has passed into automobile mythology

Le Mans 1,2,3 of 1966 (above) and 2004's tire fryer (right)

determined to produce, from scratch, a sportscar to crush the Italians on the track.

The schedule was insanely tight. Work started in 1963, with the first prototype produced early in '64. After two failed attempts, the 1966 Le Mans 24 Hours ended in a fairy-tale finish for Ford, with GT40s coming first, second and third. In three short years, the company had made Henry Ford II's impossible dream come true – and the GT40 went on to an unbroken string of Le Mans wins from 1966-69.

With its place in sportscar history sealed, it seemed that the GT40's influence would be limited to being one of the most popular shapes on the kit car scene. A detuned roadgoing version of the car had been offered by Ford from 1967, but few were sold and the rarity of these automobiles added to the model's mystique.

The rebirth of Ford's legend was

MODEL HISTORY

1963

Work starts on Ford's attempt to win the Le Mans 24 Hour race

1964

The first prototype is produced. The car, dubbed the GT40, races at Le Mans unsuccessfully

1966

GT40s make a clean sweep at Le Mans, taking first, second and third positions

1967

A road-legal GT40 is offered to the public with a detuned 306bhp engine. Not many are sold

1969

A GT40 wins the Le Mans 24-hour race for the fourth year running heralded by a modern interpretation of the GT40, a concept car shown at the Detroit Auto Show of 2003. The show car proved a massive hit and precipitated the decision to produce a road-legal production model. Symbolic of Ford's greatest achievement, it would provide the perfect centrepiece to the company's 100th birthday celebrations planned for the next year.

Just like its spiritual successor, the new car, dubbed the GT, was set an impossibly tight timescale to achieve its objective. This automobile would need to be ready in a mere 16 months. Considering that it was to be a ground-up re-interpretation of a classic racecar, that was a tall order.

The GT40 formula – a hugely powerful American V8, mid-mounted just behind the driver, clothed in low-slung race-car bodywork – was given a 21st century treatment. But this was to be a road car, so the original's 40-inch roof height (which famously helped to coin its name) would have to be stretched. In fact, the cabin's overall dimensions were enlarged, allowing taller drivers to enjoy the GT experience.

Using the latest computerized design technology, Ford designers and engineers labored to create a modern supercar to evoke the spirit of the Sixties legend. The machine they produced managed to reflect its heritage perfectly, its sleek silouhette echoing the GT40's attitude despite completely different dimensions.

At the heart of the GT is that mid-mounted 330 cubic-inch V8 which sends 550 horsepower and 500lbft to the rear wheels. This high-tech, supercharged example of the engine-builder's art drives through a six-speed manual transmission, putting an indomitable surge of urge at the driver's disposal.

The GT is breathtakingly fast – as a test driver for the American automobile magazine Car and Driver revealed in 2004. He managed a 0-60mph blast in a stupendous 3.3 seconds and recorded a

Just like its spritual predecessor the new car was set an impossibly tight timetable scorching quarter-mile time of 11.6 seconds at 128mph. Pitted against Ferrari's Challenge Stradale and Porsche's 911 GT3, the Ford wiped the floor with its opponents, the Ferrari only managing four seconds to 60mph and being 0.8secs and 13mph slower through the quarter mile. A Ford GT showed the Italians the way once more!

Despite the monstrous power, you do not need to be a hairy-chested macho man to enjoy this automobile because the GT is actually an easy car to drive. The power-assisted steering, clutch pedal and stick shift are light to operate, with the brake pedal giving access to the astounding decelerative effects of huge Brembo rotors. This is a car that can be as laid-back as a pussy cat, happy to rumble around with a few thousand rpms on the clock, but just as keen to curl its lip and go wild. Fans of great American car chases from TV and the movies will love the tire-squealing wheelspin which is available on demand, and all enthusiastic drivers will enjoy the supreme levels of grip and balance.

2004 trio (below), and GT at 205mph (right)

THE ULTIMATE FORD GT

The most successful GT40 ever is the car which won Le Mans in 1968 and '69 – chassis number GT40P/1075. Built in '68, this was one of the Gulf Racing cars finished in the team's famous powder blue and orange racing colors. With a super-light and incredibly strong aluminium-honeycomb shell, this ultimate development of the race car was capable of a 220mph top speed. When it comes to who's the daddy of all GTs, it's easy – they all are. Ford only offers this modern-day supercar in one version. Guess they think that just owning one of these cars is the ultimate in itself!

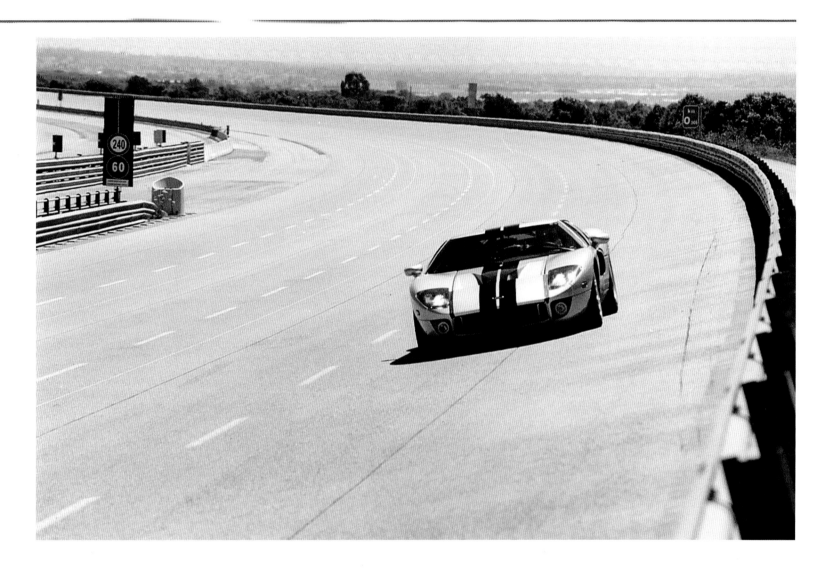

With an aluminum spaceframe and body panels, a fiberglass hood and with carbon-fiber used in the underbody aerodynamic system and the seats, modern weight-saving methods are much in evidence. And the modern attitude to comfort is also displayed in this car's interior – with standard air conditioning, adjustable seats and plenty of space, it is a million miles from the GT40's cramped cockpit. The GT's doors are deep cut into the roof, echoing the originals, and another cool feature is that, after hitting the red starter button, you can see the supercharger doing its thing as you sit in the driver's seat.

The end of this story has yet to be written, because nobody knows how long the Ford GT will stay in production. The intention was always that this "Pace car for a whole company" would be produced in limited numbers, with Ford aiming to build around 1,500 a year until demand tailed off. This is one exclusive vehicle, with a selling price of $140,000.

The Ford GT is an incredible feat of engineering built to celebrate a famous sporting achievement.

It is a true living legend.

Specification

Years built	2004 to date
Most powerful model	2004 GT
Engine type	supercharged V8
Displacement	330 cu in
Transmission	six-speed manual, rear-wheel drive
Power	550bhp
Top speed	205mph

*Ford GTs on track
in 2004 (above)
and 1966 (right)*

2004 GT opens up in the garage (above) and on the road (left)

2004 GT glamor
(above and right)

2004 GTs (above) and in wind tunnel (left)

Ford Mustang

The original Pony Car has also proved the most successful over the last forty years

Now into its fifth decade and fifth generation, the Ford Mustang was the original Pony Car. In 1964 it created a whole new muscle car class and it's the only true survivor today.

It was April 1964, mid-size muscle cars were hot, but Ford boss Lee Iacocca thought the public was ready for something else; a small, light and inexpensive sports car. That car was the Ford Mustang.

Originally conceived as a two-seater, Iacocca realized that selling the car in big numbers meant it needed to be more practical. So the Mustang that made its debut at the 1964 World's Fair in New York was shown as a four-seater convertible and hardtop. It was a huge hit, with 22,000 orders received on the first day and one million Mustangs sold within the first two years. The Mustang was a phenomenon.

And that's despite not offering

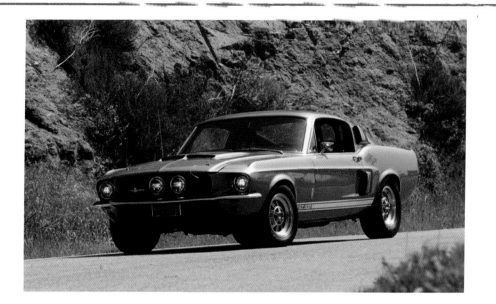

It was a huge hit, with 22,000 orders recieved on the first day and one million Mustangs sold within the first two years

1964 convertible (opposite page), 1967 GT 500 (above) and 1973 Mach 1 (right)

anything like the power of true muscle cars. At launch the Mustang came with a 170 cubic inch straight-six with just 101bhp. Ford quickly realized that this wasn't enough and by the middle of 1964 a 289 K-code V8 was offered with a much more appetizing 271bhp as standard as well as a 165bhp 260.

A fastback also arrived and with it a tie-up with racing legend Carroll Shelby. The Shelby GT-350 came with 306bhp in street specification, but the race-ready 350R weighed in with 360bhp. Stripped of any excess weight, including the back seat, the Shelby Mustang would become a legend in its own right.

To make the Mustang affordable Ford had based it on the Falcon, and by 1966 it was decided to hide its roots with an all-new instrument pack. The 260 was dropped and two versions of the 289 offered

MODEL HISTORY

1964

Mustang launched at World's Fair. 22,000 orders on the first day

1964

The first Shelby Mustang GT350 appears

1967

Mustang restyled, Shelby GT500 introduced

1968

Cobra Jet engine fitted, with up to 410bhp

1969

Mustang Mach 1 fastback goes on sale

instead. The Shelby GT-350 could now be specified with an automatic transmission and Hertz rent-a-car even bought a number to rent to weekend racers.

1967 brought the Mustang's first major restyle. It was a heavier look, but more muscular, to compete with the likes of the Chevrolet Camaro SS. A 390 big block V8 was dropped in, although the GT350 still used the 289. Shelby raised his game with the GT500, powered by a race-bred 427 packing 355bhp.

In 1968 the Mustang received the legendary 428 Cobra Jet engine. With ram air induction it produced 335bhp although everyone knew that it was really more like 410bhp. Top of the heap was the GT500KR – King of the Road – with its Cobra Jet engine and Shelby's magic worked on it.

1969's second restyle introduced the Mach 1 fastback body and saw the first Boss cars. With race-ready V8s in 302 or 429 cubic inch capacity the Boss cars were basically NASCAR racers for the road and the 429 offered a mighty 375bhp.

Sadly, 1970 saw the demise of the Shelby Cobra and by 1971 the Mustang's days as a muscle car were numbered. By the time the last of the first generation Mustangs was produced in 1973, the maximum power was just 156bhp.

1974's second generation was supposed to retrace the car's original roots as a small lightweight sports car. It didn't. The Mustang II was underpowered, too heavy and the performance was pitiful. The top flight 2.8-litre V6 took nearly 14 seconds to reach 60mph. It could hardly have been less muscular.

A year later a V8 was back with more power but compared to the previous generation it was still a slouch. Even the King Cobra of 1978 took 11 seconds from zero to sixty.

The all-new Mustang of 1979 started to regain a little ground. The car was lighter and the most powerful turbocharged four-

Hertz even bought a number of Shelby GT350s to rent to weekend racers

 1974
Mustang II unveiled, but is a slow performer and a slow seller

1974
Third generation Mustang starts to claw back lost ground

1994
30 years old and the Mustang's fourth generation arrives

2004
40th anniversary and the fifth generation Mustang arrives to celebrate

2005
Most powerful Mustang ever is launched. The Shelby Cobra GT500 has 450bhp

THE ULTIMATE
MUSTANG

The 2005 Shelby Cobra GT500 is the most powerful Ford Mustang ever. With 450bhp
from its 5.4-liter (305 cid) supercharged V8 engine it offers spectacular tire frying
performance. Ford's Special Vehicle Team was employed to fine-tune the all-round
independent suspension to give this car track-ready handling. 14-inch crossed drilled
disc brakes provide awesome stopping power and the car is finished off with Shelby's
trademark white racing stripes. It really is the ultimate Mustang.

cylinder engine (still only 143bhp) gave a
reasonable turn of speed. In 1983 a
convertible was added again after a long
absence and in '84 the Mustang celebrated
20 years with a 2.3-liter (140 cid) 174 bhp
turbo engine or a five-liter V8 (305 cid) with
a little less go. By the end of the Eighties the
V8 had its power upped to over 200bhp.

The fourth generation pony car came
in 1994 with 3.8-liter (232 cid) V6 or
five-liter (305 cid) V8 power. The restyle
was softer than before but performance was
gradually hardened up over its lifetime. It
reached its peak in 2000 with the limited
edition SVT Cobra R. Just

The latest Mustang arrived to
celebrate the model's 40th anniversary and
it's the most muscular and best-performing
pony car for three decades.

The styling is unmistakably retro,
harking back to the first cars of 1964. Power
is as plentiful as it was in the Sixties as well.
The entry-level four-liter (245 cid) V6 offers
210bhp and there's a 300bhp 4.6-liter (281
cid) V8 as well.

*2005 convertible
(right) and 1996
Mustang GT
(below)*

A five-speed manual transmission is standard, with a five-speed automatic on the options list. There's independent suspension all-round, making this the finest handling Mustang ever. Powerful all-wheel disc brakes with ABS come as standard and there's a long list of electronic driver aids as well.

Newly introduced in 2005 was a convertible version, which, unlike previous rag-top Mustangs isn't simply a chopped hardtop, but was designed as an open car from the word go. With a rigid structure its performance and handling aren't compromised like so many rag top cars.

Finally, to bring this great legend up to date Ford announced the return of the Shelby GT500 in 2005. The Ford Shelby Cobra GT500 adds a supercharger to its 5.4-liter (329 cid)V8 engine to pump out more than 450bhp.

There's a six-speed manual gearbox and suspension tuned by Ford's Special Vehicle Team. Shelby's famous white racing stripes add the final touch to this thoroughly modern muscle car.

With millions of models sold during its 40 year life, the Mustang is the ultimate muscle car success story.

Specification

Years built	1964 to date
Most powerful model	2005 Shelby Cobra
Engine type	V8
Displacement	329 cu in
Transmission	six-speed manual, rear-wheel drive
Power	450bhp
Top speed	160mph

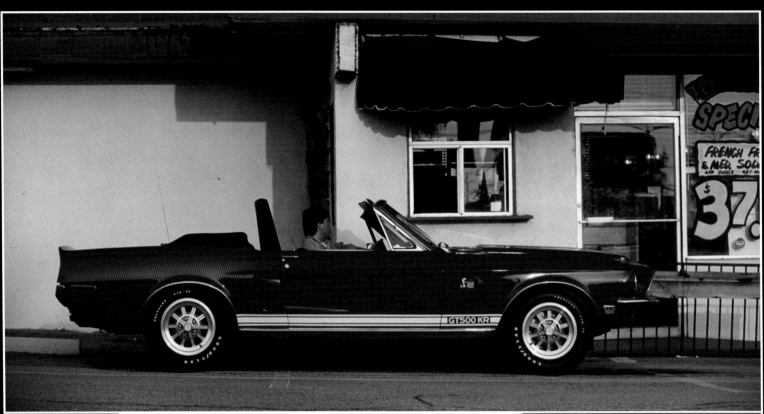

1968 Shelby GT 500 convertible (above) and 1969 Shelby GT350 (right)

1982 Mustang 5.0 (above) and 1993 convertible (left)

2000 SVT Cobra (above) and 2005 convertible (right),

2005 Shelby Cobra GT500 (above) and with original (left)

Ford Thunderbird

Now celebrating 50 glorious years, the Ford Thunderbird has been a muscle car and a luxury car, but it's always been special

The name was inspired, the look low, long and stylish, and it was a hit from the word go in 1955.

Named after the great Thunderbird of Native American legend, Ford's first two-seater sports car was intended to compete with Chevrolet's Corvette, but its eye-candy looks and high equipment levels created an entirely new market segment – the luxury personal sports car. There were 3,500 orders in the first ten days. And in keeping with the new concept the majority of the early Thunderbirds left the dealers equipped with auto transmission and the 212 horsepower version of the 292 cubic inch V8.

The 1956 design changes included flip-out side vents for better ventilation, porthole windows in the removable hardtop, improved rear quarter vision and an outside tire carrier added trunk space.

Ford also introduced its new safety

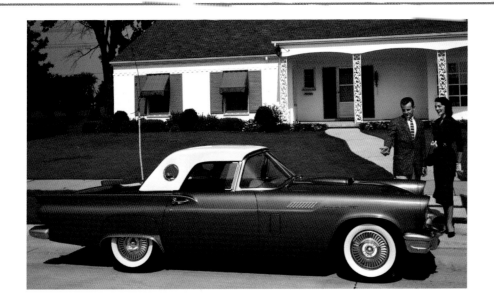

The name was inspired, the look low, long and stylish and it was a hit from the word go in 1955

2005 convertible (opposite page), 1957 (above) and 1962 (right)

idea of "packaging the passengers". Standard safety equipment included energy-absorbing instrument panel padding, a concave safety steering wheel and a shatter-resistant mirror. Safety belts were optional.

Last-minute improvements, including the addition of the optional 312 cid V8 215 horsepower engine, gave the second edition of the Thunderbird better handling and increased performance.

The '57 facelift and performance and handling improvements produced one of the most stylish and sought-after muscle cars of the '50s. New versions of the 312 Y-block V8 were offered that provided serious performance.

The E-code 312 V8 featured two four-barrel carbs and was rated at 270 bhp. The F-code 312 V8 featured a single four-barrel carb force fed by a Paxton-built McCulloch centrifugal supercharger. The F-code engine

In 1999 a two-seater concept Thunderbird was revealed at Detroit

was rated at 300 bhp, or at 340 bhp with the optional NASCAR "racing kit." It would be the last of the two-seaters.

From 1958 until 1983, Ford built a heavier, more luxurious sporty-looking but hardly sporty four-seater. The four-seat Thunderbird continued to be produced through the 80s and 90s, but the public taste for the car slowly declined, and Ford announced that the 1997 model would be the last in the line.

But the Thunderbird story doesn't end there. In 1999 a two-seater concept Thunderbird was revealed at the Detroit Auto Show. The sun-mist-yellow roadster included key styling cues from its classic 1955-1957 forebears. The concept car was a design exercise intended to gauge consumer reaction. It worked. The car proved to be wildly popular with show-goers. Two years later, Ford announced Thunderbird's return.

The 2002 Thunderbird came to market in the summer of 2001 as a limited production model aimed at 20-25,000 units of annual production. It won critical acclaim for its modern interpretation of the classic original roadster styling and was named Motor Trend's "Car of the Year."

A year on and the Thunderbird received improvements including an upgraded 280-horsepower V8. And in 2005, Ford marked the 50th anniversary of the Thunderbird with a special edition. It may not quite be the muscle car it once was, but the Thunderbird is as distinctive now as it was five decades ago.

Specification

Years built	1955 to date
Most powerful model	1957 F-code
Engine type	V8
Displacement	312 cu in
Transmission	three-speed automatic
Power	340bhp
Top speed	125mph

MODEL HISTORY

1955
Launch of Thunderbird, Ford's first two-seater sports car

1956
First restyle also brings option of 312 cubic inch V8 rated at 215 horsepower

1957
Last but most muscular and stylish of the two-seater Thunderbirds is built

1962
Sports Roadster launched with fiber-glass tonneau that converts four-seater back into a two-seater

1971
Nieman-Marcus offer 'His and Her' Thunderbirds equipped with telephones and tape players

1975

Thunderbird weighs
5,000 pounds and sold
as 'the epitome of
luxury'

1983

Introduction of the
'aero-style'
Thunderbird

1999

Thunderbird show car
wows the crowds at
Detroit Auto Show

2001

New two-seat
Thunderbird is Motor
Trend Magazine's Car
of the Year

2005

Thunderbird celebrates
50 glorious years

1965 Thunderbird (above) and 1972 (right)

2005 Thunderbird celebrates 50 years (above and left)

Mercury Cougar

The Mustang-based Cougar came in with a roar but went out with a whimper

It may have the name of a wildcat but the Motor Trend 1967 Car of the Year Mercury Cougar was still classed as a pony car. It had the look of all the Mustang derivatives with a long front end and short rear deck, but the two-door hardtop Cougar looked a bit more balanced than the Mustang as it was three inches longer.

Its equipment also took it upmarket. The XR-7 and GT came with a wood-rimmed steering wheel and bucket seats, and the GT took the Cougar into the muscle car league with its 390 cubic inch 335bhp V8. The GT included firmer suspension, with stiffer springs and shocks, and power front disc brakes. The 390 engine had hydraulic valve lifters and a four-barrel Holley carb.

The Cougar GT-E was new for 1968 and signalled an increase in performance with a 390bhp 427 cubic inch V8. But this engine made the car nose-heavy and it

The GT took the
Cougar into the
muscle car league
with its 390 cubic
inch 335bhp V8

*1969 Eliminator (opposite
page and right) and 1968
hardtop (above)*

suffered from a distinct lack of grip off the line. Insurance company complaints led to this engine being replaced with the new and lighter Ford 428 cubic inch engine rated at a low 335bhp. But, according to many experts at the time, the actual output was closer to the 390 horses of the 427. The 428 had a longer piston stroke than the 427 which made it easier to meet increasingly stringent exhaust emission regulations.

1968 also saw the introduction of the Cougar XR-7G. The 'G' stood for Gurney – stock car race ace Dan Gurney who drove a Mercury briefly in 1968. In spite of its go-faster looks, in reality the car was no faster than the GT-E. Curiously the 'G' package was available with any Cougar. The add-ons included a fiberglass hood scoop, a racing mirror, an optional sunroof, spoke pattern wheels, four-pipe exhaust and special 'G' emblem badges. Not many 'G' Cougars

Real performance was added to the Cougar with the 1969 Eliminator

were made, so very few exist today.

Real performance was added to the Cougar in the middle of 1969 with the addition of the aggressively named Cougar 'Eliminator'. Although the 1969 Cougars were longer, wider and somewhat heavier the availability of the 428 Cobra Jet with Ram Air got the Cougar, with its longer wheelbase, quicker off the line than the Mustang – though the quarter-mile mile times were about the same. With a black grille, front and rear spoilers, side stripes and day-glow blue, orange and yellow body colors, the Eliminators looked the business. The 335bhp 428 also got the Eliminator off

the line to 60mph in 5.6 seconds and ran the quarter-mile in 14.1.

Mercury certainly reckoned that bigger was better for the Cougar in 1970. It also had a new look that further reflected its Mustang origins. The Eliminator stayed in the line-up and came with a 429 V8 with Ram-Air and a rated output of 375bhp.

By the beginning of the 1970s the era of the Detroit muscle car was nearing its end. Sales of the performance Cougars declined. In 1971 the Cougars were bigger again and the Eliminator was eliminated from the line-up. Cougar luxury rather than performance was the marketing word. The 429 cubic inch V8 was still on offer, but would be dropped for 1972.

1973 saw the last of the Cougar pony cars. The hottest engine was the mild 351 V8 with 266bhp. So the wildcat Cougar went out with a miaow rather than a roar.

Specification

Years built	1967 to 1973
Most powerful model	1970 Eliminator
Engine type	V8
Displacement	427 cu in
Transmission	three-speed automatic
Power	375bhp
Top speed	127mph

MODEL HISTORY

1967

Cougar is Motor Trend's Car of the Year

1967

Cougar GT has 390 cubic inch 335bhp V8

1968

Cougar GT-E launched with 390 bhp 427 cubic inch V8

1968

Dan Gurney inspired XR7-G fails to inspire many sales

1969

Stringent emission regulations lead to long-stroke 428

1969

Cougar 'Eliminator'
launched with 335bhp
long-stroke 428 Ram
Air Cobra Jet V8

1969

Eliminator runs the
quarter-mile in
14.1 seconds

1970

Eliminator scores with
375bhp 429 cubic inch
V8 with Ram-Air
induction

1971

Luxury pushed instead
of performance as sales
of Cougar decline

1972

Last of the Cougar
pony cars as output
drops to 266 bhp

Mercury Cyclone

The warmed up Comet was set up as a rival to the budget-priced Road Runner

The Mercury Cyclone was the hot version of the Mercury Comet. First announced in January 1964, its sporty features included bucket seats, an instrument console, chrome trim bits for the 210bhp 289 cubic inch V8, and chrome wheel trims that gave the impression – from a distance – that the car had chrome wheels. The Cyclone was a budget performer, but it was a performer nonetheless.

For 1966 the Comet was based on the larger Ford Fairlane. The wheelbase was now 116 inches and the front track was wider, making room for Ford's big block engines. Good news.

Both hardtop and convertible body styles were available. There was also a GT option that included Ford's new 335bhp 390 cubic inch V8. Buyers could dress the car up with a fibreglass hood with a fake scoop and GT stripes and badges. The standard transmission was a three-speed manual, with options of a four-speed manual or three-speed automatic.

The Cyclone and Cyclone GT continued in 1967, although for some reason the 390 cubic inch engine was downrated at 320bhp. The 1968 car had a facelift and a new fastback coupe body style was added.

This proved to be a wise move. The fastback outsold the notchback by a factor of 20 to one. The convertible was dropped. The most powerful engine of 1968 was the 390bhp 427 cubic inch V8. This was dropped after just a few months and replaced with Ford's legendary 428 Cobra Jet V8, with 335bhp.

1969 saw the introduction of the Cyclone CJ (Cobra Jet), aimed directly at the Plymouth Roda Runner in the low-price

MODEL HISTORY

1964
Mercury Cyclone introduced as sporty derivative of the Comet

1966
Cyclone based on larger Ford Fairlane makes room for big block engines

1967
New fastback body-style outsells notchback by 20 to one

1969
Cyclone CJ introduced – aimed at low-price performance car market

1972
Production of Mercury Comets and Comet Cyclones ends

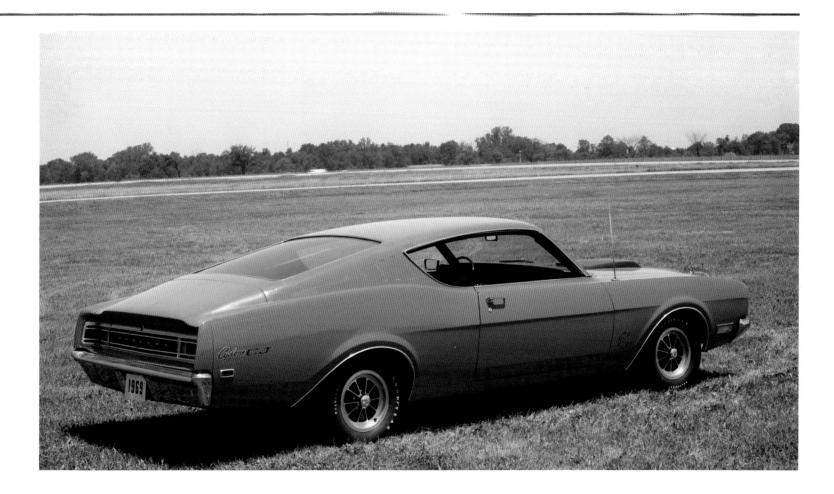

performance car market. The CJ standard engine was the 335bhp 428 cubic inch. The CJ also came with a four-speed manual transmission, a competition handling pack – and most curiously, a bench seat.

The hottest Cyclone of the year was the Spoiler II with improved aerodynamics aimed at success on the NASCAR circuit. Spoilers came in two levels of trim , named after NASCAR heroes Dan Gurney (blue roof and stripes) and Cale Yarborough (red roof and stripes). Both came with a 351 four-barrell V8 not, as many hoped, the Cobra Jet. Sales of just 519 units hardly seemed worth the effort.

Further hot but re-styled and larger Cyclones continued through 1970, inlcuding a handful of BOSS 429-powered cars, but were dropped in 1971 as the muscle car era slowly came to an end. The last Cyclones were made in 1972.

Specification

Years built	1964 to 1972
Most powerful model	1969 CJ
Engine type	V8
Displacement	427 cid
Transmission	four-speed manual
Power	390bhp
Top speed	127mph

The hottest Cyclone of 1969 was the Spoiler II with improved aerodynamics aimed at success on the NASCAR circuit

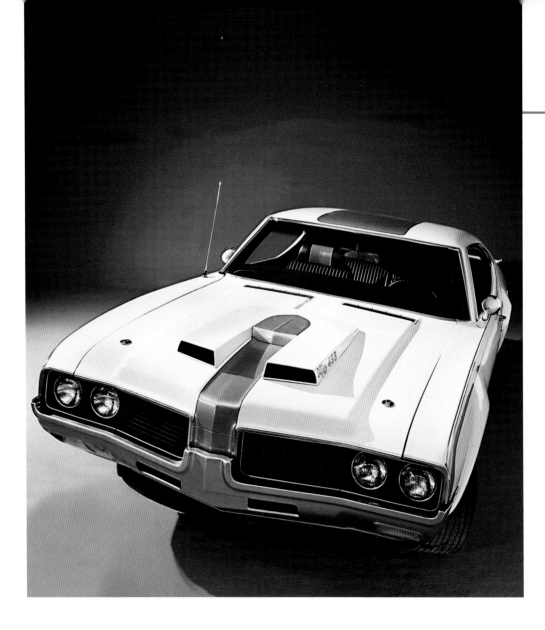

Oldsmobile 442

The 442 was originally a performance package rather than an actual model. The numbers signified a four-barrel carburator (4), a four-speed manual transmission (4) and dual exhausts (2), with these sporty ingredients offered on Oldsmobile's Cutlass. The recipe for the 442 was to change over the years, but the name stuck and was to become the byword for Olds' muscle cars.

The Cutlass 442 was launched after the Pontiac GTO had paved the way. Oldsmobile wanted a piece of the action, whacking its biggest-hitting power unit into its midsized chassis. At 330 cubic inches, this V8 came modified with all the performance equipment specified by police departments for pursuit cars. The deal also included heavy duty shocks and springs plus a rear stabilizer bar.

The first model-year of the 442 was a confused affair, with the package being available on the cheaper F-85 as well as the Cutlass. Oldsmobile hadn't got its marketing strategy together, so less than 3,000 442s were sold in 1964. Not a promising start, but better was to follow...

For 1965, Oldsmobile got its act together with its advertizing, which gave the 442 a more youthful image and greater sales success. The performance package was more

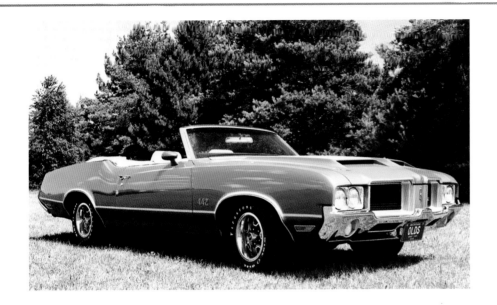

This V8 came
modified with all
the performance
equipment specified by
police departments

*Awesome Olds/Hurst
(opposite page),
442 convertible (above)
and coupe (right)*

attractive too, with a new 400 cid V8 replacing the old unit, bringing power up to 345bhp. The new 442 pack also improved on the class-leading handling, with heavy duty shocks and springs, plus front and rear stabilizer bars along with fat tires.

Clothed in fresh sheet metal, the 1966 model Cutlass 442 emerged with a new option – the first opportunity to have triple carburators fuelling the engine. The set-up was smooth and lifted power output to 360bhp, while suspension upgrades increased handling standards even further.

The tri-carb option didn't last long, with a GM ban on such set-ups forcing Oldsmobile to seek alternative methods to maintain power output in 1967. They did it with the W-30 package, a "forced air induction system" with special air ducting, plus an uprated camshaft and springs.

The 442 of 1968 saw the famous name finally became a model designation in its own right. '68's biggest news was the

> The W-30 achieved its highest power output thanks to a balanced, blueprinted 455 V8

Hurst/Olds. Originally a one-off marrying of the 442 with the 390 horsepower 455 cid V8 from Oldsmobile's Toronado, a limited run was sanctioned by the company. Capable of 0-60mph in 5.4 seconds, only 515 were made in '68, making them prized collector's items today. The Hurst/Olds returned for 1968, with a new colour scheme and extravagant bonnet scoops, although it was slightly detuned to 380bhp.

In 1970 GM's ban on engines over 400 cubic inches in midsized cars was lifted, allowing Oldsmobile to offer its 455 cid V8 in all 442s as standard. The Hurst/Olds was now dropped, not to reappear until 1972.

The W-30 achieved its highest ever power output, thanks to a balanced, blueprinted and generally hotted-up version of the 455 V8. 1970 also saw the arrival of a new option, the Rallye 350 – its 310 horsepower engine wasn't exceptional, but the exterior treatment was, with bright yellow paint – even on the bumpers and wheels!

It was a last joyful fling at outrageous visual effect and hedonistic performance, because from 1971 the 442 faced the same power-capping factors as all muscle cars.

From '72, the 442 merely denoted a handling and appearance package for any Cutlass. The Hurst/Olds was reissued, but with only 300bhp it was a shadow of its former self – and by '73 it was down to a 250. After '73, Olds dropped out of the performance market and although the 442 name later reappeared on many models, none of them could match the originals.

Specification

Years built	1964 to 1973
Most powerful model	1968 Hurst/Olds
Engine type	V8
Displacement	455 cu in
Transmission	four-speed manual, rear-wheel drive
Power	390bhp
Top speed	130mph

MODEL HISTORY

1964
442 option first offered on Oldsmobile's Cutlass model, with 310bhp, 330 cid V8

1965
New 400 cid, engine joins 442 package, generating increased power at 345bhp

1966
Tri-carb option gives 360bhp. 442's reputation for handling enhanced with suspension upgrade

1968
442 becomes a stand-alone model name. Top-dog Hurst/Olds introduced with 390bhp

1970
GM lifts ban on engines over 400 cid

1870

Hurst/Olds dropped as its 455 cid V8 becomes the 442's standard power unit

1871

Power-restricting legislation heralds dwindling performance

1971

Even the W-30 is down to 300bhp

1972

442 is now only a hanndling and styling package

1973

The last of the true 442s is built

Oldsmobile Toronado

A front-drive muscle car? Nobody would have believed it until the Toronado

The Toronado was a truly radical machine. Never mind the amazing styling, the Toronado was the first and only true front-wheel drive muscle car.

The story started in 1966 when Oldsmobile launched the largest front-wheel drive car ever made. It received a fantastic reception from press and the public. Motor Trend magazine named the Toronado their Car of the Year.

With a wheelbase of 119 inches this was one big beast, and at 4,366 pounds it was no lightweight, but Olds gave it serious horsepower to compensate for that. Under that long hood was a 425 cid V8 that turned out 385 hp. And that was plenty.

To avoid too much weight over the front end, the torque converter was mounted behind the engine whilst the gearbox sat under the engine's left bank.

It was an ingenious piece of engineering and laid the groundwork for the American automobile industry's switch from rear to front-wheel drive.

The Toronado's styling was no less revolutionary. It was the work of GM design boss William L Mitchell and he really made this Olds stand out from the crowd. Boldly flared wheelarches, fenders that jutted out aggressively from the front, headlamps hidden away and a fastback tail made this one striking car.

The Toronado was a big hit in its first year of production with more than 40,000 models sold.

A '67 restyle was limited to a new front grille, whilst 1968 saw the Toronado tamed a little. Those stand-out fenders were

MODEL HISTORY

1966
Oldsmobile launches the biggest ever front-wheel drive car

1966
Motor Trend names the Toronado Car of the Year

1968
Restyle tames the Toronado a little

1970
But not for long, GT launched with 400bhp

1971
Second generation emphasizes luxury over muscle

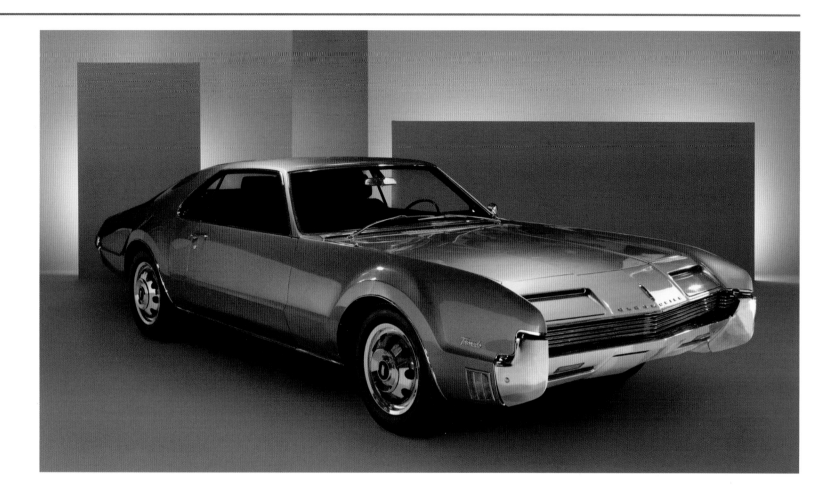

reigned in and Olds' new split grille was added, whilst under the hood a new 455 cubic inch 375bhp V8 was fitted.

In '69 a longer tail was added and so too was an optional, but ugly and quite unpopular vinyl top.

1970 saw a more significant change, with fixed headlamps replacing the concealed ones and the addition of a 400bhp GT version. With a special cam and torque converter the GT could hit zero to sixty in just seven and a half seconds. You could spot a Toronado GT thanks to its twin exhausts, slotted rear bumper and gold paintwork with black stripes.

During the five-year production run more than 120,000 series one Toronados rolled out of the factory. The series two that

followed was a shadow of its former self, emphasizing luxury over performance, so it's the original that is the collectors' item. Just ask Jay Leno, he's a proud Toronado owner.

Specification

Years built	1966-1970
Most powerful model	1970 GT
Engine type	V8
Displacement	455 cid
Transmission	three-speed automatic
Power	400bhp
Top speed	135mph

With a special cam and torque converter the GT could hit zero to sixty in just seven and a half seconds

Plymouth Barracuda

It beat the Mustang to market, but it would be some years before the 'Cuda could be considered a true pony car

A true muscle car it ain't – but the 1964 Plymouth Barracuda did beat the Mustang to market by two weeks. Its other claim to fame was its huge wrap-round rear window, said to be the largest single piece of glass ever used on a production car. Initially the Plymouth sales pitch concentrated on the Barracuda's looks and convenience and the most sporty engine on offer was a 273 cubic inch 235bhp V8.

The Formula S Barracuda, introduced in 1965, was supposed to be a performance car. But it wasn't. The most powerful engine on offer was still the 273 cubic inch 235bhp V8 and it wasn't any faster than standard models. There was a facelift in 1966 and the distinctive 'Fish' badges were added.

Then, in 1967, things began to change. The Barracuda had a redesign and it truly joined the ranks of the pony cars. Notchback and convertible body styles were

Plymouth Barracuda 2-Door Sports Hardtop

The 1964 Plymouth Barracuda beat the rival Ford Mustang to market by two weeks

1970 'Cuda (opposite page), advert for the '65 (above) and 1970 'Cuda Hemi (right)

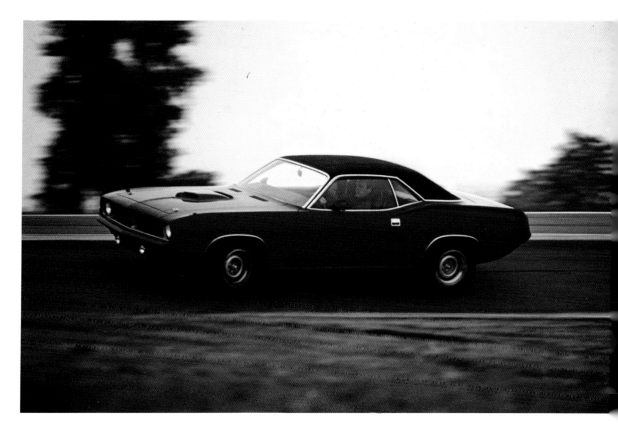

added to the original fastback. Plymouth even thought about adding their 280bhp 383 cubic inch engine to the options list. The thought didn't make it to production – the engine was too large to fit the power steering pump under the car's hood.

A 383 cubic inch V8 was squeezed into the 1968 car and coincided with an abbreviation of the name. The Formula S Barracuda became the sportier-sounding 'Cuda with no less than 300bhp on tap. The zero to 60mph dash was accomplished in a reasonably rapid 7.5 seconds. But, despite the power upgrade, the quarter mile was managed in the hardly competitive high 15s.

1969 saw more attempts to make the 'Cuda faster and more competitive with its rival muscle cars. On offer were the 383 V8 with 330bhp and the most powerful engine in the Plymouth stable, the 440 cubic inch, triple carb 390bhp V8 – the largest engine

When the engine shook, which it did a lot, so did the Shaker

ever offered in a pony car. With a weight distribution of front/rear 57/43 per cent and no room for power-steering the car was a pig to handle. With drum brakes all-round and no power-steering it was also difficult to stop quickly in a straight line. However the engine helped define the 'Cudas sportier image – zero to 60 took 5.6 seconds and the quarter-mile an impressive 14.01 seconds.

The 'Cuda finally made it in 1970. It was given a new platform, the E-body shared with the new Dodge Challenger. The 'Cuda's wheelbase was two inches shorter, though its overall dimensions were the same. No less than five V8s were on offer,

the most muscular being the 390bhp 440+6 and the mighty 425bhp 426 Hemi. 'Cudas with these engines had tougher performance suspension and the Hemi had a feature that quickly became a muscle car icon – the 'Shaker' hood scoop – so-called because it was fixed to the engine and protruded through a hole in the hood. When the engine shook, which it did a lot, so did the Shaker.

There was also a special 'Cuda for 1970 – the AAR. It was sparked by 'Cudas raced by Dan Gurney's All-America Racers in the Trans-Am races. But unlike the Boss 302 Mustang and the Camaro Z28, the AAR 'Cuda was built as a street rod. An estimated 1,500 AARs were built.

Then in 1971, tougher emission laws came into force. The Hemi was dropped and the remaining engines were de-tuned. Sales dropped almost as quickly as the engine power and the 'Cuda finally died in 1974.

Specification

Years built	1964 to 1974
Most powerful model	1970 Hemi 'Cuda
Engine type	V8
Displacement	426 cu in
Transmission	three-speed automatic
Power	425bhp
Top speed	130mph

MODEL HISTORY

1964
Plymouth Barracuda beats Mustang to market by two weeks

1966
Barracuda 'fish' emblems introduced. Most powerful engine has just 235bhp

1967
Notchback Barracuda joins ranks of pony cars. Performance Formula S version available

1968
383 cubic inch 300 horsepower V8 available in Formula S Barracuda

1969
440 cubic inch, triple carb 390 horsepower V8 is the largest engine ever offered in a pony car

1989

1969 'Cudas sportier
image re-defined – zero
to 60 takes 5.6 seconds
and the quarter-mile
14.01 seconds

1970

'Cuda makes it as a
true pony car as notch-
back introduced

1970

Hemi gets a feature
that quickly becomes a
muscle car icon – the
'Shaker' hood scoop

1970

AAR 'Cuda is the first-
ever production car
with rear tires larger
than front tires

1974

Final 'Cuda rolls off
the production line

Plymouth Prowler

Plymouth's concept car made real may not have had much muscle, but its hot rod styling made it a hit

The Plymouth Prowler looks like a flight of fantasy, a concept car that has just rolled off a show podium. And basically, that's what it is. The Prowler is one of those rare beasts – a concept car that made it into production.

A modern interpretation of the street hot rods of the Fifties, the Prowler made its debut at the Detroit Auto Show of 1993. Jaws dropped, flashbulbs popped and nobody really thought that Plymouth's parent company, the Chrysler corporation, would ever build it. It was just too wild. But they reckoned without Chrysler president Bob Lutz, whose support for the project was pivotal in getting the Prowler signed off and into production.

It would take until 1997, after four consecutive show-stopping performances at Detroit, for this automobile to finally hit the street. But when it did, it remained remarkably true to its original concept. A

The Prowler looks like a flight of fancy, a concept car that has just rolled off a show podium

2001 Prowler (opposite page and above with custom trailer) and 1999 model (right)

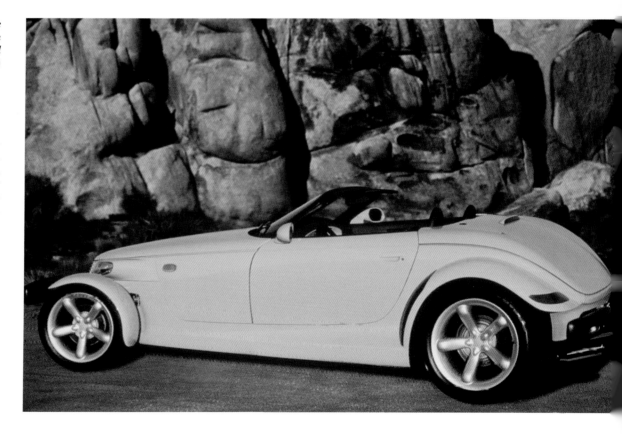

two-seater roadster with a manually-operated soft top and the sort of radical looks only normally found at hot rod clubs, it was a unique, off-the-peg custom car. For the guy who wanted a street rod but also wanted comfort, reliability and modern automobile attributes, it was a godsend.

The car was the most aluminum-intensive car produced in North America at the time. Most of the bodywork was constructed of this lightweight metal, as was the suspension, helping to reduce weight as much as possible. And it needed to keep itself trim because, unlike its spiritual forebears from the Fifties, it was not powered by a huge V8.

The power unit was the same 3.5-liter (213 cid) V6 found in Chrysler's sedans, producing 214bhp. In the (relatively) light-weight Prowler, its performance was brisk rather than roadburning. But who cared

It remained the same dream machine that inspired so many auto enthusiasts

when you were at the wheel of something this outrageous and getting all the looks?

The Prowler was given a bit more go to accompany the show when a new aluminum V6 started taking care of business in 1998. Power rose to 253bhp, making this a lively but well-mannered roadster. A four-speed Autostick transmission had manual override, allowing the driver to shift up and down the ratios by tapping a stick shift. The ride quality was firm and performance-oriented, although it would be softened down during its years of production.

Originally only available in purple, a whole slew of retro hot-rod colors gradually became available over the car's five-year lifespan, including yellow, orange and deep candy red. Just to underline the fact that this was a car for extroverts, if you didn't already know.

Luggage space was minimal and there wasn't even room to stow a spare tire. The solutions were to offer a matching trailer to give somewhere to stash the valise (an option which 20 per cent of buyers took up) and fat, run-flat tires.

The Prowler ceased production in 2002, and apart from the original engine being upgraded, few major changes were made to the model during its life cycle.

It remained the same roomy, leather-upholstered, electric-windowed, drop-top dream machine that inspired so many auto enthusiasts to take it to their hearts and onto their driveways.

Specification

Years built	1997 to 2002
Most powerful model	1998 onwards
Engine type	V6
Displacement	213 cu in
Transmission	four-speed Autostick
Power	253bhp
Top speed	125mph

MODEL HISTORY

1993
Prowler is first displayed at Detroit and rocks the show

1994
Prototype is taken to hot rod shows to gauge reaction

1996
Official go-ahead for the model is announced at Detroit

1997
First production Prowlers built alongside the Dodge Viper

1998
All-aluminum 3.5-liter (214 cid) V6 introduced, giving 253bhp

1999

New shock absorbers and springs give a smoother ride

1999

Black and red two-tone Woodward Edition unveiled. Only 150 made

2000

Black Tie silver an black special edition released. Only 163 made

2001

Plymouth brand is discontinued, Prowler is rebadged as a Chrysler

2002

The Prowler cruises off into the sunset as the model is axed

2001(above) and
1999 (right)

1998 model (above) and 1997 (right)

Plymouth Road Runner

The back-to-basics Plymouth Road Runner was one of the most successful muscle cars ever. Beep Beep!

When the Road Runner hit the scene in 1968, it made the biggest impact on the market since Pontiac's GTO back in '64. Four years of muscle car development had resulted in expensive, luxury-laden automobiles, so with the Road Runner, Plymouth decided to get back to base principals. It aimed to create a no-frills road-burner with lots of bang for as few bucks as possible.

For a mere $2,896, the American public could purchase a base-level Road Runner, equipped with a 383 cubic inch V8 pumping out 335bhp. The chassis, based on the Plymouth Belvedere, was beefed up with uprated suspension, while the interior was right back to basics with a simple bench seat and rubber matting replacing carpets.

It was an impressive package for the price, but for an extra $714 you could put a fearsome 426 Hemi under the hood of your

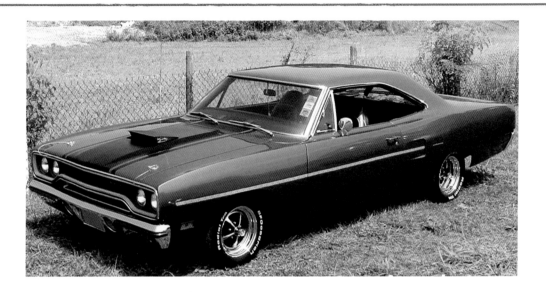

To go with the decals, there was even a horn that went "beep beep" in cartoon Road Runner style

1970 Super Bird (opposite page), 1969 (above) and 1974 Road Runner (right)

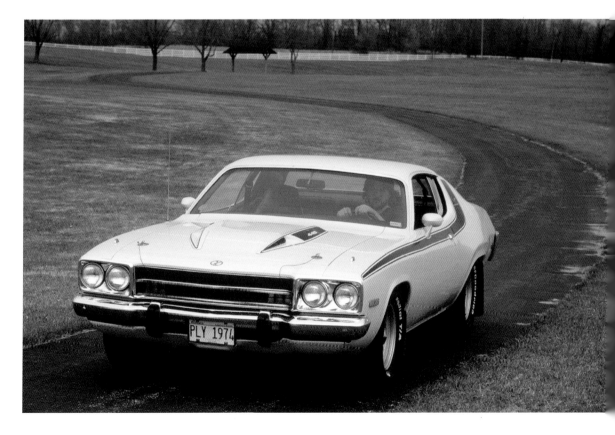

Road Runner. For just $3,610 you could own an automobile that could do 0-60mph in 5.3 seconds and tear up a quarter-mile in the low 13s.

And what a cool car! Plymouth created the perfect youth-oriented image for its new creation. The company paid Warner Brothers a reported $50,000 to use their famously fast cartoon bird as the car's logo – and adopted its name too. To go with the decals, there was even a horn that went "beep-beep" in cartoon Road Runner style.

Just like its animated namesake, the car was a runaway success. Plymouth expected to sell 2,500 in its first year, but pretty soon it was the car every kid wanted and 45,000 flew out of the dealerships.

Its success prompted Plymouth to expand the range in 1969, bringing in a convertible to bolster the existing hardtop and pillared coupe. Two new 440 cid V8s

A powered trap door on the hood popped up revealing a shark cartoon

included the "440 + 6", a triple-carb job which gave Hemi-like acceleration for almost half the price.

Another feature with hip graphics gave the Road Runner a psychological edge. In 1970, the Air Grabber Hood appeared on the options list. A powered trap door on the hood popped up when operated by a dashboard switch revealing a shark cartoon and the words "Air Grabber". A cool way to demoralize the opposition at the stoplight!

Some say the ultimate Road Runner, the Super Bird, was a cartoonish creation too. Built in 1970 to emulate the racing success of Dodge's Daytona, it featured similarly outlandish aerodynamic bodywork. The wedged nose and huge rear spoiler, even taller than the Daytona's two-foot high affair, guaranteed attention.

NASCAR rules required car makers to build one car per dealer for it to be eligible for the race series and Plymouth ended up making nearly 2,000 Super Birds. But despite success on the track, 1970 remained the only year it was produced.

The next year saw a stripping-down of the Road Runner range. The Hemi was legislated out of existence and the two-door hardtop was the only body style on offer.

The original Road Runner ceased to exist in 1974. The name continued as a trim package on a budget car.

The end came in 1980, with the final Plymouth Road Runner far removed from the 'cheap, fast thrills' philosophy of its original incarnation.

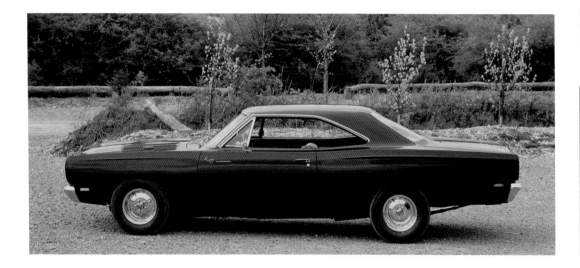

Specification

Years built	1968 to 1980
Most powerful model	1970 Hemi Super Bird
Engine type	V8
Displacement	426 cu in
Transmission	four-speed manual
Power	425bhp
Top speed	160mph

MODEL HISTORY

1968
First Road Runner is a very animated package offering big bangs for low bucks

1969
Range expanded with two new V8s and a convertible added to the line-up

1969
Road Runner sales double

1970
Air grabber hood offered as an option

1970
Ultimate Road Runner, the Super Bird, is created with race-oriented aero styling

1970

2,000 Super Birds sold

1971

Hemi engine legislated
out of existence

1974

Original-generation
Road Runner
discontinued. The name
continues as a trim
package

1977

Road Runner uses first
engine management
computer

1980

The Road Runner
reaches the end of the
road, a shadow of its
former self

The star of 1970, Plymouth Road Runner Super Bird

Beep Beep!
Super Bird

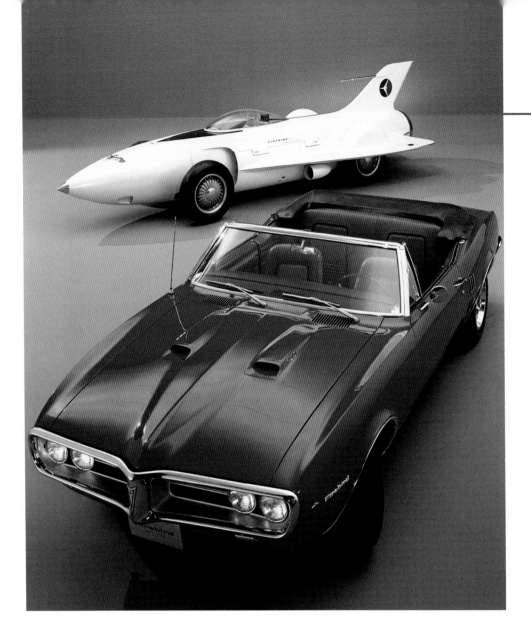

From Smokey and the Bandit to Knight Rider the Pontiac Firebird Trans Am was an American hero for 35 years

Pontiac Firebird

The Firebird has a special place in the history of American performance vehicles. It enjoyed continuous production from its inception in the muscle car boom of the Sixties to the modern era, setting a record only the Chevrolet Corvette can equal. When the final car rolled off the line, the Firebird had notched up an amazing 35-year lifespan.

The story started in 1967, when the first Firebird's distinctly beaky hood and GTO-style tail lights successfully established a separate identity to the Chevrolet Camaro that it was based on. Initially available with six different engines, most buyers went for the V8s which included the 400 cubic inch, 325bhp unit from Pontiac's GTO.

As it evolved through four distinct generations of development, the Firebird would go through numerous changes, but a big V8 would always feature as the top performance option. The power peak came in 1970, with the Ram Air V, a special-order 440 cubic-inch motor kicking out 500bhp. The engine formed part of the Firebird's top performance package – called the Trans Am, after the US race series. The name would become an American automobile legend.

The collapse of the muscle car market led GM bosses to consider axing the Firebird, but Pontiac fought to save the 'bird

When the final car rolled off the line, the Firebird had notched up an amazing 35-year lifespan

First (opposite page) and last (above) of the line and 1976 Trans Am (right)

and it won a reprieve. It was a corporate decision that was to provide big rewards.

The early Seventies were tough times for American performance cars, but the Firebird blasted away the clouds with its new Super Duty 455 cubic inch V8. "Super Duty" was the name given to Pontiac's race-ready engines in the Sixties and the Super Duty 455 made the Firebird the only serious performance car on the market. This street-legal, race-prepped engine was rated by the company at 310bhp, although experts agreed it actually produced nearer 370.

When the Firebird Trans Ams which packed these fearsome engines received a new decal, their iconic status was sealed. A huge image of an eagle with its wings outspread took up most of the hood, it screamed a rallying cry to performance car fans throughout the US, giving the Trans Am massive credibility and supercool status.

As the Seventies wore on, however, further power restrictions took their toll,

It got all the best lines performing as KITT in Knight Rider

with the Super Duty engine phased out in '75 and the 455 V8 falling by the wayside in '76. Despite the drop in maximum power, the Firebird still managed to score sales of over 100,000 for the first time in 1976. A serious boost for the car's image came the next year, when Burt Reynolds drove a black and gold Special Edition Trans Am in the hit movie Smokey and the Bandit. Pontiac made the most of the car's new-found fame, issuing a flood of Special Edition Trans Ams which helped to almost double the Firebird's overall yearly sales in 1978.

Another starring role reaffirmed the Firebird's popularity in 1982, when it got all the best lines performing as "KITT", David Hasselhoff's talking techno-car in Knight Rider. The model's top engines had been seeing a steady decrease in power throughout the Seventies and early Eighties, but this third-generation, hatchback-bodied 'bird now saw a gradual increase in output. 1987 saw a new 210bhp 350 cid V8 and in '89 a 250bhp turbocharged V6 powered the special 20th anniversary edition Trans Am.

The fourth and final generation, from 1993-2002, were the fastest and most powerful since the glory days of the muscle car boom. Top dog was a 5.7-litre V8 which developed from 275 to 320bhp during 1993-98. But with customer tastes for performance cars changing, the model didn't live long into the 21st century and its passing into history was ushered by a 35th anniversary Firebird – a specially-painted Trans Am.

Specification

Years built	1967 to 2002
Most powerful model	1970 Ram Air V
Engine type	V8
Displacement	400 cu in
Transmission	three-speed automatic
Power	500bhp
Top speed	130mph

MODEL HISTORY

1967
First Firebird, based on the Camaro chassis from Pontiac's fellow GM brand, Chevrolet

1969
'Trans Am' first introduced as a performance package. It becomes symbolic of Pontiac muscle

1970
Second-generation 'bird gets the 500bhp Ram Air V engine as an optional power unit

1973
Golden Eagle spreads its wings on the Trans Am's hood

1976
The Firebird ceases to pack 455 V8 power

Trans Ams from 1967 (above) and 1971 (right)

1999's Firebird (above) and 2003 special (left)

Pontiac Grand Prix

It was the least extrovert of Pontiac's muscle cars, but it still offered plenty of peformance

Although tastefully low-key in styling, the Pontiac Grand Prix sported a good few muscle car credentials in its launch year of 1962. Not least was the special build of 16 cars equipped with the 421 cubic inch 370bhp Super Duty V8 that took the Grand Prix to 60 miles an hour in a respectable 6.6 seconds. Just one of these specials is believed to survive. Otherwise muscle car fans made do with the 425-A Trophy V8 engines and a maximum output of 348bhp.

The Grand Prix's interior was fairly sporty with bucket seats, floor shift, and an instrument console with a tachometer. Chequered flag badges front and rear gave a nod to the car's name and race aspirations.

The Grand Prix was given a new look for 1963. Less sculpted lines and a 'Coke-bottle' waist together with a new roof-line and an unusual concave rear window gave the car a very distinctive profile. The rear

Although tastefully
low-key in styling, the
Grand Prix sported
a good few muscle
car credentials

*1965 in Paris (opposite page),
1971 (above)
and 1962 (right)*

window was to stay as a Grand Prix feature until the 1968 model year. The high power engines for 1963 were two 421 cubic inch V8s, one with a four-barrel carb that put out 353bhp – the other was a 370bhp version called the HO Tri-Power. The 1963 car proved to be popular with car buyers with a total of nearly 73,000 sold.

Following the Detroit trend, the Grand Prix got bigger and heavier for its next incarnation in 1965 – and it was also moved more towards the luxury market segment. And horror of horrors, a bench seat was on offer to replace the original bucket seats and console. Engine options changed too. Power actually increased with new engine features such as better gas flow through new design manifolds and cylinder heads. The 389 base engine had 256bhp and Tri-Power version increased this to 338. The 421 four-barrel carb also made 338bhp and

The 1969 redesign is reckoned to be its finest incarnation

the two Tri-Power engines put this figure up to 353 and 376bhp respectively.

The beginning of the end for this generation of the Grand Prix came in 1966 as sales of the manual transmission cars fell to under 1,000.

The Grand Prix got even bigger in 1967, and it was the only year a convertible version was on offer. The car now looked massive and to cope with the increased weight the base engine was now a 400 cubic inch V8 with 350bhp – although a low-power 265bhp unit could be substituted. The most powerful V8 was the 421 cubic inch engine which put out 376bhp. 1967 was also the year that exhaust emissions had to meet Federal smog regulations, and the introduction of first-phase safety equipment. The Grand Prix now came with a collapsible steering wheel, dual-circuit hydraulics and optional disc brakes. But the car's size now put off buyers who were looking for smaller cars – and sales continued to fall.

It wasn't until another re-design in 1969 that the buying public took to the Pontiac Grand Prix in reasonable numbers. The car looked sharper and more stylish, almost like a stretched pony car. The wheelbase was three inches shorter. The car handled better and with its new 428 cubic inch 390 horsepower V8 it ran the all-important quarter-mile in 14.1 seconds.

The Pontiac Grand Prix continued in production until 1974, but the 1969 redesign – kept in the main until 1972, is reckoned to be its finest incarnation.

Specification

Years built	1962 to 1974
Most powerful model	1968
Engine type	V8
Displacement	428 cu in
Transmission	three-speed automatic
Power	390bhp
Top speed	129mph

MODEL HISTORY

1962
Pontiac Grand Prix introduced with 425-A Trophy V8 engines and a maximum output of 348bhp

1963
Re-style with lower roofline and concave rear window

1963
Sales of 73,000 prove re-styled car's popularity

1965
The 421 Tri-Power engines put out 353 and 376 bhp respectively

1966
Sales of manual transmission cars fall to under 1,000

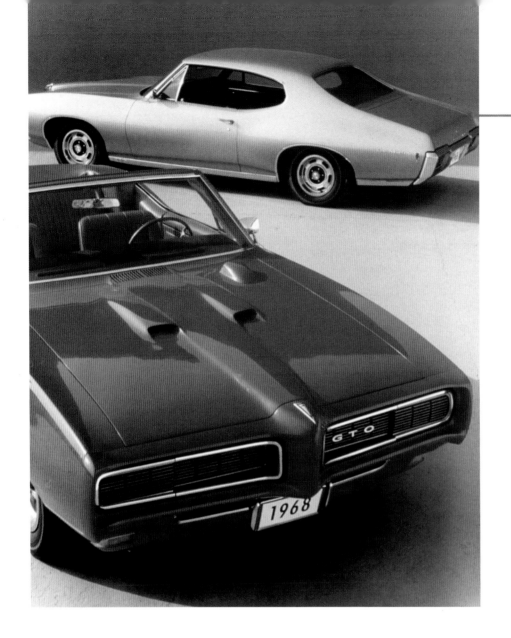

Pontiac GTO

In many eyes the Pontiac GTO was the first true muscle car with full-size power in its mid-size shell

This is where it all began. In 1964 Pontiac saw a gap in the market. There were plenty of full-size cars packing a serious punch, but the mid-size market was down on performance and prestige as a result of a GM ban on factory-backed racing and a limit of 330 cubic inches on standard engine size.

In a cunning move Pontiac got around these restrictions by offering the LeMans GTO (Gran Turismo Omologato) package as an option on the Tempest model.

It was distinguished from the regular Tempest thanks to air scoops on the hood, special redline tires, heavy duty suspension, three-speed floor-shift tranny, chromed air cleaner and rocker cover and a special 'engine-turned' instrument panel plate.

With a 389 cubic inch V8 from the Bonneville under the hood, the GTO offered 325bhp in standard trim. The Tri-Power kit replaced the standard four barrel carburator with three double-barrel carbs and upped that power to 348bhp.

With a 0-60mph time of 7.5 seconds and able to run the standing quarter-mile in les than 15 seconds the GTO quickly gained legendary status. Sales went through the roof. Pontiac hoped to sell 5,000 in the first year, but in the event more than 32,000 found owners. This car was a sensation.

Pontiac hoped to sell
5,000 in the first year
but more than 32,000
found owners

*1968coupe and convertible
(opposite), 1965 (above) and
1964 (right) two- doors*

For '65 Pontiac capitalized on the astonishing success of the GTO with a major front and rear restyle. The nose now incorporated stacked headlights from Pontiac's full-size models. Engine power was upped with the standard 389 offering 335bhp and the Tri-Power a mighty 360bhp. The bonnet scoops that were just styling ploys on the '64 model could now be used to feed a ram air system that could be bought from dealers.

A year later and the GTO became a model in its own right. There was yet another restyle to give the car a more sculptured Coke bottle look, but there were no changes under the hood.

By 1967 GM had banned multiple carburators on all models except the Chevrolet Corvette, so Pontiac needed another solution. In went a bored-out 400 cid V8 that came in four states of tune. There was Economy with just 255bhp, Standard with 335bhp or HO (High

The GTO was reborn in 2004 as a sleek-looking two-door

Output) and Ram Air, both with 360bhp.

The GTO was restyled once again for 1968 and sat on a new 112-inch wheelbase. The innovative rubber Endura bumper was now fitted and hidden headlamps were added to the options list. The Economy and Standard engines both gained 10bhp but the HO and Ram Air stayed at 360bhp.

1969 was the year of the Judge. This special edition GTO was named after a phrase on TV's 'Laugh In' this GTO featured wild paint colors and a hefty rear spoiler. Two new Ram Air engines offered 366 and 370bhp. The GTO was getter faster by the year.

1970 saw yet another restyle, with four exposed headlamps and a softer look all over. A new 455 engine was offered that matched the Ram Air's 360bhp, but the coolest trick of 1970 was the VOE option. This Vacuum Operated Exhaust system employed a hot rod technique that opened the exhaust to give more power. The driver pulled a knob on the dash and back pressure in the exhaust was cut, thus giving more go and more noise into the bargain. Sadly GM bosses soon stamped on this option.

Over the next three years the GTO suffered like all GM muscle cars with restrictions on horsepower and emissions. The GTO ceased to be a model in its own right in 1972 and production ended in 1973.

The GTO was reborn in 2004 as a sleek-looking two-door. And with 400bhp from its six-liter (364 cid) LS2 V8 it's a true modern muscle car and not just a namesake.

Specification	
Years built	1965 to 1974, 2004 to date
Most powerful model	2005 GTO
Engine type	V8
Displacement	364 cu in
Transmission	six-speed manual
Power	400bhp
Top speed	150mph

MODEL HISTORY

1964
Pontiac fits a Bonneville engine in the Tempest, creating the GTO

1965
First restyle and power increased to 360bhp with the Tri-Power option

1966
GTO becomes a model in its own right

1967
Mutiple carbs banned, new 400 cid V8 installed

1968
Another restyle features indestructible Endura bumpers

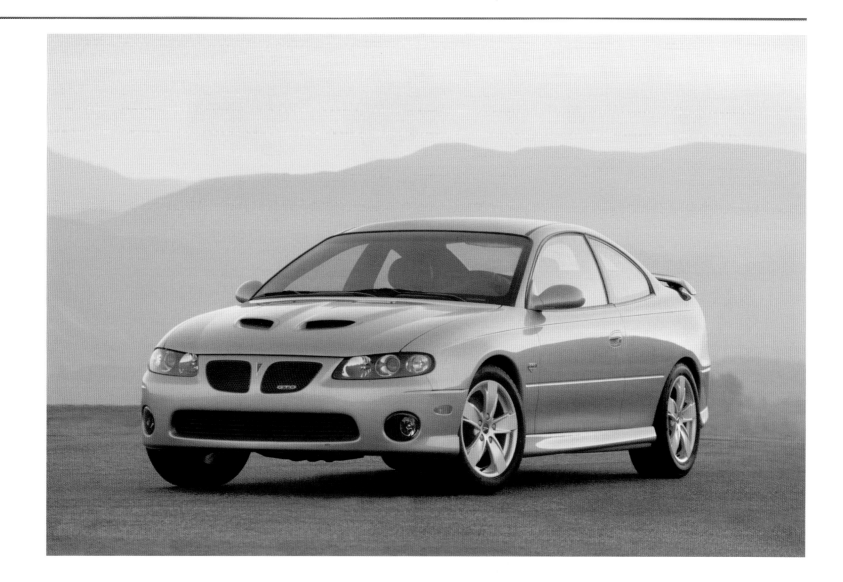

1969

The year of the Judge –
the wildest-looking
GTO yet

1970

Sneaky VOE option
makes GTO faster syill,
but annoys GM bosses

1971

Horsepower rates
reduced to meet
tough emissions rules

1974

GTO production ceases

2004

A legend lives on with
new 400bhp GTO

1964 convertible (above) and 1970 coupe (right)

1967 convertible (above) and 1974 coupe (left)

Shelby Cobra

When Carroll Shelby teamed American V8 power with a lightweight British sports car he created a legend that still lives on today

Created by one of the most charismatic characters in American sportscar history, the Cobra has attained mythical status amongst automobile fans the world over. Larger-than-life Texan Carroll Shelby was the man who synthesized US muscle and English style so perfectly that the car is still built today – over 40 years after its original inception.

Shelby, a successful sportscar racer and previous winner of prestigious European endurance race, the Le Mans 24 Hours, was forced to retire from the track in 1960 due to ill-health. With a vision of producing a sportscar combining a lightweight European chassis with American V8 power, he set about making his dream a reality. The opportunity came the next year, when English manufacturer AC cars agreed to Shelby's idea of muscling-up its Ace sportscar, and a deal was struck.

Luckily for the Texan, Ford had just

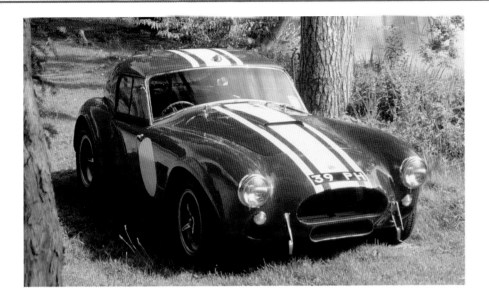

The Cobra has attained mythical status amongst automobile fans the world over

1962 (opposite page), 1964 Le Mans (above) and 1964 road car (right)

developed a new small-block V8 but had no serious performance model to put it in. After successful negotiations, the recipe was written for one of the most spine-tingling sportscars ever made.

During a couple of months in early 1962, the cute little Ace was transformed into a hair-raising beast at Shelby's California workshop. What emerged was a classic expression of muscularity in metal – the original Cobra roadster, the fastest production car ever made at that time. With explosive acceleration from 0-60mph in a breath-taking 3.9 seconds, the car won rave reviews from motoring journalists and its curvaceous lines wowed the crowds at American auto shows. Shelby's visionary concept had struck a major chord in the hearts of sportscar fans.

The first Cobra packed a 256 cubic inch engine, but its creator's insatiable desire

The need to conform to race regulations led to the most powerful Cobra being sold

for power and performance meant that pretty soon a 289 cubic-inch version of the Ford V8 was installed. And it didn't stop there. Shelby campaigned the Cobra successfully in American and European race series – and it was his desire to win that produced the most awesome Cobra of all.

The need to conform to race regulations led to the most powerful road-going Cobra becoming available to the public. Deciding to shoehorn an even bigger Ford V8 under the hood to keep it competitive in production endurance racing, Shelby went for the 427 cubic-inch option. By 1967, 31 competition cars equipped with

this engine had been finished – not enough to qualify the model for racing. His only option was to fit windscreens to unsold Cobras that had already been built and offer them for sale to the general public in order to meet the quota.

The 427 Cobra was born – one of the fastest-accelerating production cars of its day, with vital statistics of 0-60mph in 4.5 seconds, a standing quarter-mile in 12.4 and 165mph top speed. That's blisteringly quick, even by today's standards!

The last 427 Cobra was built in 1967, but the model wasn't dead and buried. Shelby reprised his classic sportscar in different guises throughout the Eighties and Nineties – and his company still makes them to order today. It's a testament to the allure of the car which, with its combination of V8 power in a lightweight chassis, many feel started the whole muscle car movement.

Specification

Years built	1962 to date
Most powerful model	1965 427
Engine type	V8
Displacement	427 cu in
Transmission	four-speed manual
Power	410bhp
Top speed	165mph

MODEL HISTORY

1960
Carroll Shelby retires from racing with a dream to build the ultimate sportscar

1962
First Cobra is built from AC Ace chassis and Ford 256 cid V8

1963
The race car wins the United States Road Racing Championship

1964
Hardtop Cobra Daytona Coupe wins GT class at Le Mans 24 Hours

1965
The 427, featuring tube frame and aluminum body, is unveiled

1965 Cobras for road and track (above and right)

1969 289s (above and left)